The Humility Imperative

Why the Humble Leader Wins in an Age of Ego

ANDREW KERR

ISBN: 978-1-4834-6816-7 (sc)
ISBN: 978-1-4834-6818-1 (hc)
ISBN: 978-1-4834-6817-4 (e)

Library of Congress Control Number: 2017905489

Lulu Publishing Services rev. date: 04/21/2017

DEDICATION

For my family—the source of both
my confidence and my humility.

CONTENTS

CONTENTS

He has told you, O mortal, what is good; and what does the Lord require of you but to do justice, and to love kindness, and to walk humbly with your God?

Micah 6:8

PREFACE

I've always thought the best books were stories of survival. Survival against great odds, against the forces of nature, or against the worst humanity has to offer. Books of fiction offer amazing flights of fantasy and reveal truth, but why fabricate mythical heroes when the real ones are so readily accessible? Give me a true story about a lone traveler lost at sea, marooned in the desert, or trapped in an artic winter, and my mind opens to the miracles that occur when people are pushed to their limits and find previously unknowable strength, grit, and determination. These are my kind of stories.

Imagine my delight when I had the chance to meet one of history's all-time survivors, Everest climber Beck Weathers. I was very familiar with Weather's story first chronicled in Jon Krakauer's bestseller, *Into Thin Air*. The book tells the tale of May 10, 1996 when ten individuals became trapped in a hurricane-force wind as they tried to descend from Everest's peak. Split up, blinded, and overwhelmed by the storm, seven climbers and three of the best mountaineering guides in the world would perish. Krakauer's story is a tragedy, and by all accounts Beck Weathers should have been victim number eleven on that ill-fated day.

Weathers was a climber of only ordinary physical prowess. However, he possessed extraordinary ability to grind his mind and body through the oxygen-starved, slow torture of big mountain climbing. On the final push to Everest's summit, Weathers had become temporarily snow-blind due to the effects of altitude and recent eye surgery. He promised expedition leader Rob Hall he would rest for a half hour to see if his eyesight improved. If not, he was to wait for Hall to return on the descent rather than proceed down the slope alone. A man of his word, he would pay a terrible price for the promise he made. Although it seemed impossible to imagine when he swore his oath, Rob Hall would never make the descent.

After hours of waiting for Hall and passing up multiple opportunities to descend with other climbers, Weathers became entrapped in the blizzard with several other climbers. Although just a few hundred feet from the safety of their high camp, the small party became disoriented and was forced to hunker down to try to ride out the storm. As the winds raged, the climbers fought to stay warm. They kicked each other, hugged each other, and screamed into the wind for help. The climbers knew staying awake was truly a matter of life and death. Dozing off above twenty-five thousand feet in subfreezing temperatures meant rapid hypothermia and eternal sleep. In recorded history, no one had ever fallen into a hypothermic coma at that altitude and survived.

LEARNING HUMILITY

When I was a young boy, my grandfather would take me on long drives in southern Georgia to visit once-a-month flea markets. These outdoor bazaars included hometown hobbyists, local artisans, and frustrated farmers looking to pick up a few dollars selling their wares, along with bargain hunters hoping to find an overlooked treasure. My grandfather was always an enthusiastic collector. From stamps and coins to old toy cars, he would meticulously organize his various collections and preserve each item carefully in tissue paper and plastic. His favorite thing to bring on these weekend forays was his collection of antique, handmade tools. He had dozens of custom hammers, screwdrivers with wooden handles, and larger specialty pieces like hatchets and reapers. He loved to carefully organize the displays and then spend the afternoon chatting up customers by asking them to guess the origin and function of his most exotic implements. I don't recall us ever selling very much, and usually my favorite part of the day was when my grandfather would announce it was time to pack up and head back home.

The ride home normally meant a treat of some sort as a reward for my hard work as his trusted lieutenant. We would stop at the Varsity in downtown Atlanta and get a pair of their signature frosted orange milkshakes. My grandfather also had a love of words, and on the way home we would play a game. It was a vocabulary contest where he would pick a word—usually several levels above my reading proficiency—and ask me to give him the definition. Because I typically had no idea of the possible meaning, I would instead try to come up with a clever definition that sounded something like the word itself. For example, if he asked me to define the word "ubiquitous," I would pause for a moment before confidently declaring that ubiquitous meant, "when you bite someone and they taste squishy." If my answer was somewhat humorous, he would give a hearty laugh before explaining to me the real definition. It was a silly game, but for some reason I still remember many of the words I learned on those long drives. In fact, one of the words I can recall learning was the word "modesty."

> **Modesty**: the quality or state of being unassuming or moderate in the estimation of one's abilities.

I had never heard this word before and couldn't immediately come up with any clever definition. After struggling in silence for a few moments, my grandfather explained carefully that it meant, "not bragging or showing off, even when you can." I remember being puzzled, thinking perhaps I still didn't understand the meaning, but his definition has always stuck with me.

Growing up the son of a successful automotive dealer in Atlanta, I had the opportunity to observe leadership up close from an early age. My father was an extremely hard worker who learned the car business step by step and took nothing for granted. He was aggressive, blunt, and had a passion for serving customers. If you could keep up with his pace and match his intensity, you would be rewarded handsomely with his loyalty. If you couldn't, watch out!

One of the early lessons my father taught me about leadership was that ego was one of the most dangerous things in business. As a general rule, auto dealers are shrewd negotiators who tend to think highly of themselves. My father worked elbow to elbow, competing amongst these hard-bitten types for years, and he had seen many dealers both rise and fail spectacularly. His personal formula for success seemed to come down to three things: (1) show up every day (even Saturdays); (2) compete like hell; and (3) get to daily mass every morning. Growing up, I was convinced it was the first two items on the list that helped my father achieve his success, and it was only years later I would come to realize the importance of the third one.

WHY HUMILITY?

I have always been fascinated by leaders and what made them succeed or fail. As a young person, I would collect quotes from great leaders, carefully cataloguing their wisdom in loose-leaf notebooks. Throughout my early career, I had the privilege of working across a variety of industries spanning business, sports, and politics. In the first ten years of my career, I coached D1 college football, served under a marine general at the Department of Homeland Security (DHS), and worked extensively with senior leadership at the nation's largest for-profit health care company, the Hospital Corporation of America (HCA).

As my career evolved, I was given the opportunity to lead talented teams, and I quickly discovered that leadership required continuous improvement and self-study. I am a firm believer that the best way to learn something is to try to teach it back to someone else. To this end, I adopted an annual goal to study different aspects of leadership and then share what I had learned across the organization. I soon became a certified facilitator and began teaching dozens of leadership development classes annually on topics such as change management, managing up, and coaching for high performers. In late 2014, I was searching for a new topic to focus on for the following year and came across a random blog post that caught my attention.

Over the next year, I read and researched as much as I could find about humility and tried to understand how it may provide unique advantages to leaders. I was initially pulled in because I realized that characteristics like modesty and humility where in short supply among many leaders I had observed but also plentiful in the very best ones. In truth, I became borderline obsessed with the topic. Whenever I picked up a biography or a book on leadership, I immediately flipped to the index to see if the author mentioned humility (regrettably, most do not). If I did happen to find a reference or mention of humility in a popular article or blog post, I stored it away for later study. I regularly searched Twitter for the hashtag #humility.

All this is not to claim that I am an expert on humility (what irony that would entail) but only that I have done my best to explore it from the inside out, to catalogue its essence, and to examine it from all the angles. I also readily recognize whenever you pour this much time and effort into a particular topic, you run the risk of becoming a little too personally vested in it. You can easily become a rabid evangelist who proclaims "humility" as the answer regardless of the question. However, I became strongly convinced that humility could provide tremendous value to leaders. I had seen the humble way exceptional leaders approached problem solving and felt the depth of their character during difficult moments. I also realized this value has been largely ignored in our modern empowerment culture. Humility has somehow become confused with weakness or timidity. I found it frustrating to observe companies spending millions annually to develop leaders toward success but never addressing the unique problems that occur once they arrive. As I continued to observe the deleterious effects of ego within the workplace, I became convinced it was time to reinvent an old concept.

A Modern-Day Resurrection

Weathers' compelling firsthand account of his survival is masterfully told in *Left for Dead*. As I quickly devoured his story of survival, I also found myself captivated by a deeper question. Why was he ever on that mountain to begin with? It was a question that had been asked of every Everest climber since Sir Edmund Hillary, but few had ever come up with anything better than his trite "because it's there." Thankfully, Weathers took the time to explore this question and to reveal with refreshing honesty that his motivation came from a much darker place.

Despite being a successful pathologist with a beautiful family, Weathers had repeatedly been dogged by depression. Over the years, it would surge or recede depending upon circumstances, but he had never summoned the courage to acknowledge it fully or even to reveal his struggles to his closest loved ones. Instead, he had stumbled upon an unexpected cure. The hard physical exertion and extended outdoors exploration mountaineering required became an elixir, lifting the black cloud he lived in constant fear of. Over time, this prescription would be become an addiction. It took him to spectacular destinations all over the world but also further and further from his wife and young children.

When Weathers experienced his miracle on the mountain, he recalled with frightful clarity for the first time that the one thing he couldn't live without was his family. He clung to a vision of them as he awoke on Everest and somehow stumbled his way into high camp. Given up for dead hours earlier, Weathers had a modern-day resurrection. His miracle would come with an awful price. Due to severe frostbite, he would lose both hands and his nose. He would endure more than a dozen surgeries to repair his broken body. His big mountain-climbing days were over.

When he finally made his dramatic return home, his wife revealed that prior to his resurrection, she had sworn she would divorce him upon his return from Everest. Over the years, his selfish pursuit of mountain summits had left his wife wondering for weeks on end whether he would return. In anguished dreams, fearing the worst, she would cry herself to sleep. Out of combination of love and pity, Peach decided she would give Beck a year to recover and told him if he was a changed man at the end of one year, she would not divorce him.

Weathers now regularly shares his story to audiences and is open and honest about his motivations, the cost, and what he has learned. Often he is asked—knowing fully the cost, would he do it all again? He admits that the first time he was asked the question, he thought it was rather stupid. Does he miss having hands? Would he rather not have frozen to death on the mountain alongside good friends and fellow climbers? Yes, of course. But today he puts it this way: "Even if I knew exactly everything that was going to happen to me on Mount Everest, I would do it again. That day on the mountain, I traded my hands for my family and for my future. It is a bargain I readily accept."

For me, it is the last part of Weathers's story that is the most important. Unintentionally, he had lost perspective on what was most important in his life. Fighting against his demons, he brought enormous pain to his family and nearly lost them. Only when he was humiliated, maimed, and literally frozen to death did he recover his perspective. Yet he declares unequivocally that he would do it again. I believe him. But in the back of my mind, I told myself, "There has to be a better way." The story of this book is about finding that better way.

This book is intended for leaders of all types who openly struggle to balance the thin line between healthy confidence and destructive pride. My goal is to demonstrate how humility is the greatest tool available to help leaders keep perspective and avoid the types of catastrophic mistakes that occur all too often. Let's get started.

Chapter 1

HUMILITY'S IMAGE PROBLEM

Plenty of people wish to become devout,
but no one wishes to be humble.
—La Rochefoucauld

Maurice was born into a lower-middle class Jewish family in New York, New York, on May 4, 1925. His father, a candy store owner, would die when Maurice was only six years old, leaving his mother to move upstate and later remarry a dairy farmer. Although Maurice was born into the Roaring Twenties, his formative years were spent scraping through the hard times of the Great Depression on a ramshackle farm at the foot of the Catskills near Liberty, New York. At age seventeen, Maurice escaped his impoverished hometown by lying about his age and enlisting in the elite Army Rangers. He was shipped to England for training and would soon see action at Omaha Beach on D-Day. Later in the war, he participated in the liberation of the Dachau concentration camp. After World War II ended, he attended the University of Miami majoring in prelaw and then earned a law degree from New York Law School in 1950. However, just as he was set to begin his legal career, the Korean War broke out, and he quickly found himself stationed in South Korea. He eventually rose to the rank of captain and later received a Bronze Star for meritorious service. After returning from Korea, he chose to go into business rather than law, and at the age of thirty-four, he was named the youngest vice president in history at a large domestic insurance agency.

Maurice possessed an indefatigable work ethic and a tough, bare-knuckle style when confronting competitors. He loved to travel and soon developed a knack for international expansion. When his more conservative competitors looked at a foreign market and saw too much risk, Maurice would jump in with gusto. When he took over as CEO, annual revenues were a substantial $915 million, but he grew them to a staggering $165 billion. He transformed his company into a behemoth that made it all the way up to number nine on the Fortune 500. He also became a billionaire, reaching as high as number forty-seven on Forbes's annual list of the world's richest individuals.

Maurice's track record was also remarkably consistent and sustained. He wasn't a corporate hatchet man, slashing jobs for a short-term stock boost; instead, he focused on consistent growth. Eventually, he would become the longest tenured Fortune 500 CEO, spending an astonishing forty years in his position. By nearly any standard, Maurice's story was a wildly successful one, a tale about overcoming a tough childhood, rising through the ranks, and becoming a billionaire. It is a very American story. One of tenacity, grit, and triumph. But unfortunately, the story doesn't end there.

THE LOGO OF LEADERSHIP

What are the qualities and skills required to become a great leader? If I posed this question to a large audience, there would be a variety of answers, and we could quickly compile a list. Great leaders are bold. They are able to chart new courses and guide their teams through the tumultuous change processes needed to break new ground. Great leaders are tenacious; they frequently work harder and drive further than their peers and competitors. They tend to be highly intelligent and are often gifted communicators. Great leaders also develop their people and get the best out of their teams. Leaders need to be courageous and also know when to listen. At the end of the day leadership is a bottom-line business, and great leaders are those who execute a given mission, often against great odds, and ultimately bring success to their organizations.

In many ways, the question is both uncomplicated and infinitely dense. While the list may be long and varied, there are certain qualities that we commonly associate with historically great leaders and still look for today.

On the other hand, other attributes simply don't fit. While we may want to date somebody with a good sense of humor, we don't typically think of leaders as funny. Compassion and sensitivity are qualities that make for an excellent friend, but they are not adjectives you normally see splashed across the cover of *Forbes* magazine. Nobody roots for a favorite team to draft the most polite linebacker. Regardless of which side of the aisle you vote on, the most gracious or down-to-earth politician has won few recent campaigns. Although all admirable, these qualities aren't likely to appear on the traditional leadership checklist. Why not?

WINNING BEYOND THE BOARDROOM

True success today is also multidimensional, and Maurice's success extended far beyond the corporate boardroom. Due to his heavy international travel and knack for networking, he developed a reputation as one of the most knowledgeable figures in international business. In fact, his perspective was so sought after that the CIA regularly debriefed him after he met with various foreign heads of state. He was also generous. He made large charitable contributions within his local community and served on several nonprofit boards, chairing multiple philanthropic endeavors[i]. While serving as the director for the powerful Council on Foreign Relations, his feisty temperament was on full display when he publicly shot down Iranian president Mahmoud Ahmadinejad. When Ahmadinejad made comments that attempted to deny the Holocaust, Maurice seized the floor, telling the crowd, "I went through Dachau in the war and saw it with my own eyes!"

By almost any measure, Maurice was a highly successful business leader. He possessed every one of the standard leadership qualities that we might put on our list. Intelligent ... check. Bold ... check. Tireless work ethic ... check.

These qualities drove him to the very top of his profession and made him seem a classic rags-to-riches American success story. But unfortunately, this isn't a success story. It turns out that as a leader, Maurice was missing one crucial quality, a critical element that unfortunately is left off most leadership checklists. Some consider it old-fashioned or irrelevant; others think that it is incompatible with powerful positions. In fact, I suspect that Maurice himself would have struggled to understand how this little quality would have benefitted him. Although Maurice is his given name, this tremendous leader is better known as Hank Greenberg, the now infamous former CEO of the American International Group (AIG), whose risky growth strategies almost singlehandedly bankrupted the world economy during the global financial crisis of 2008.

THE BIG QUESTION

As a student of leadership for as long as I can remember, I have always been fascinated by figures like Hank Greenberg. He was a titan of industry, dynamic and aggressive—the type of leader who faced tough competition and got results. Greenberg served his country honorably, grew a hugely successful multinational company, and gave back to his community. But the question that haunted me was, where did he go wrong? How did somebody this smart, who gave so much effort and sustained his success for so long, take such a disastrous fall—one that nearly took the entire global economy with him?

Greenberg didn't suddenly become stupid. He didn't lose his edge as he got older, and I don't believe he was driven too far by insatiable greed. But he did ultimately fail, spectacularly and catastrophically. Was it a lack of knowledge? A failure to recognize changing conditions? Perhaps it was a more personal failure of character. While these questions are valid to explore, the most disturbing realization is that the type of failure Greenberg experienced is not uncommon. In fact, it is all too common. While Greenberg's fatal flaw manifested itself on a global scale, the reality is that similar failures of leadership happen every day across every industry in every cultural context. In the wake of the disaster, many questioned what could have been done to prevent the collapse. What are top leaders missing that could prevent future disasters? The answer may be smaller than you think.

THE MISSING INGREDIENT

Before we seek out the missing ingredient, let's begin with a question. Read the descriptions of the two leaders below and pick which leader you would rather have running the company you work for.

Executive A: engaging, innovative, dynamic, aggressive, smart, compelling, persuasive, and charismatic

Executive B: quiet, modest, reserved, shy, understated, mild-mannered, forgiving, and gracious[ii]

Having posed this question to various audiences for the past two years in leadership development classes, I have found that the honest response is that the vast majority would strongly prefer Executive A. For better or worse, engaging, charismatic leaders dominate corporate boardrooms and fulfill our prototypical image of what a leader should be. We are naturally attracted to their confidence, creativity, and uncompromising drive to succeed. These leaders are known to get results, often through the sheer force of their personalities or genius. The popular press reinforces this image and is quick to crown successful CEOs as business icons and global brands. We live in an era that celebrates confidence and moxie; not surprisingly, our leaders are a reflection of this. Growing up with the pervasive influence of social media, impressionable millennials and digital natives appear comfortable with self-promoting leaders who might have been judged vain and shallow by older generations. While we may occasionally lament that leaders appear more attention seeking and narcissistic, the vast majority of us still strongly prefer this to the more reserved manner of Executive B.

Against the popular dominance of charismatic leadership, however, evidence suggests that trust in leadership, whether it be in business, politics, or sports, has sunk to record lows. The 2015 Edelman Trust Barometer shows a global decline in trust, and the number of countries with trusted institutions has fallen to an all-time low among the informed public. Their research indicates that 60 percent of countries distrust the media. Trust in government remains low in nineteen of the twenty-seven markets surveyed. Trust in business is also below 50 percent in half of those markets. It seems that there is a fundamental mismatch between our expectations of leaders and what they actually deliver. While we may be attracted to their charisma, we also distrust their leadership on some level.

While the trust deficit between leaders and followers today is concerning, I would contend that a critical quality is missing from Executive A that breeds this fundamental distrust. That missing quality, which is in short supply among today's charismatic leaders, is humility. The word "humility" originates from the Latin word *humilis*, meaning "grounded," "from the earth," or "low." But today humility is often equated with being meek and lowly. It is seen as synonymous with weakness and submission. In our self-actualizing society, it can even be seen as opposed to the value and excellence of the individual. While we may see value in the "gracious" or "modest" style of Executive B, above all we want to see strength and confidence in our leaders. Words like "meek" and "submissive" simply do not show up on any leadership checklists. But then how is humility even relevant for leaders in today's hypercompetitive global economy?

This fundamental ambivalence toward humility in leadership

is nothing new. Looking back through history, we have always had trouble fitting humility into our standard leadership profile. On the one hand, the poet Tennyson once said that humility is "the highest virtue, the mother of them all."[iii] However, philosopher Frederick Nietzsche was an outspoken critic equating humility with a type of "slave morality" and viewing humility as "a strategy used by the weak to avoid being destroyed by the strong."[iv] Humility has long been considered virtuous if narrowly confined to religious leaders, but in more secular, competitive pursuits it has always been tougher to reconcile.

However unfounded, our stereotype of humble individuals may lead us to believe that:

- **Humble people are doormats**. We believe humble people won't stand up for themselves so they can be run over by more confident or aggressive competitors.
- **Humility equates to poor self-esteem**. We reason that if you don't believe in yourself, then nobody else will. If people are humble because they have poor self-esteem, then humility is not a virtue to attain but rather the natural result of their inherent lack of self-worth.
- **Humble people are poor salespeople.** If people aren't willing to promote themselves, you certainly don't want to put them in a position to defend your company or champion your brand. We think humble people are allergic to the limelight or unwilling to speak up, so we label them as poor salespeople.
- **Humbled by failure.** Lastly, we reason that people who are humble got that way by being humiliated by various setbacks and failures in life. We want to be led by successful people with proven track records of success, not serial failures.

Ironically, the old-fashion value of humility seems to have a modern-day image problem. Others may say humility simply doesn't sell very well. If you look broadly across the consumer products industry, you will find no shortage of products specially named to associate their brand with supreme confidence. In the clothing industry, there are multiple urban clothing lines utilizing the name "Swagger." The Arrogant Bastard Brewing Company's top seller annually is their signature Arrogant Bastard Ale. As far back as the 1980s, Proctor and Gamble sold us on the idea that you should "Raise your hand if you Sure" for their popular deodorant. More recently, Old Spice has remixed that campaign with their top-selling Swagger deodorant for men. Admittedly, humility has never sold a stick of deodorant, and it seems that rock stars known for their humility rarely make the cover of *Rolling Stone*.

But why do we undervalue humility to such an extent? It is a problem deeper than any Madison Avenue makeover. Broader cultural shifts are at work, and there are three fundamental reasons humility is consistently underappreciated in contemporary culture:

- **Prize success over failure**. In our image-conscious culture, we worship at the altar of success and see little value in even discussing failure. When reviewing a resume for a job opening, we want to see an unblemished record of success. There should be evidence of progressive, high achievement and uninterrupted forward movement. There may be a slight allowance for the mistakes of young people, but we have little tolerance for adults who make mistakes and even less for leaders. We select people for leadership positions because we believe the adage that past performance is the best predictor of future success. We place so little value in failure that is it rarely discussed even among close friends—it is taboo, impolite, and best avoided and moved past. A culture that chooses to either stigmatize or ignore failure therefore has little regard for the lessons it can teach and the humility it can produce.
- **The power of perception**. We have all heard the relatively modern truism "perception is reality." This typically means if you display an image of success and confidence, then people will perceive you as such, and thus the image

eventually becomes reality. Greek mythology christened this phenomenon the "Pygmalion effect." The popular modern corollary is the more simply stated "fake it until you make it." We have somehow come to fully embrace the idea that people are mostly competent and credible and that if we could only somehow shed our self-limiting beliefs and display more confidence, success would appear on our doorstep. While "fake it till you make it" is catchy, it seems to imply that all we need to be successful is better acting lessons. Consider, what are the long-term implications for businesses and governments if leadership ranks simply become populated by the best fakers or those who simply look the part?

- **Self-Esteem above all else.** The term "helicopter parent" has come to mean an overly protective caregiver who is always nearby to swoop in and prevent his or her child from stumbling or failing. As parents, we often go to great lengths to build up our children's self-esteem, seeking to assure them they are special and unique and too often shielding them from the consequences of their own actions lest their youthful confidence be damaged. While the practice has been decried, the reality of participation trophies is still widespread. However, self-confidence isn't developed when somebody else praises you with positive affirmations. Self-esteem results when an individual is able to accomplish something on his or her own. Clay Christensen, in *How Will You Measure Your Life*, powerfully recounts the time his mother made him sew up the holes in his own socks. This simple act of earned competence inspired him to believe in himself and his ability to solve bigger problems.

It is easy to overgeneralize broad cultural trends, but few would argue that humility has become less valued over the past few decades. In her best-selling book, *Quiet—The Hidden Power of Introverts*, Susan Cain says, "We moved from what cultural historians call a culture of character to a culture of personality. During the culture of character, what was important were the good deeds that you performed when nobody was looking. Abraham Lincoln is the embodiment of the culture of character, and people celebrated him back then for being a man who did not offend by superiority. But at the turn of the century, when we moved into this culture of personality, suddenly what was admired was to be magnetic and charismatic."

Author and columnist David Brooks echoes this sentiment in *The Road to Character* when he declares, "We have seen a broad shift from a culture of humility to the culture of what you might call the Big Me, from a culture that encouraged people to think humbly of themselves to a culture that encouraged people to see themselves as the center of the universe."[v] Brooks says that today, we relentlessly preach the "gospel of self-trust," and our broader stories and popular cultural narratives teach us that all we need to do is to "follow our hearts" to be successful.

If we put these ideas together into a formula, it would go something like this. Strive for success above all else—this is the societal imperative. In order to be successful, constantly hone the image of success. Minimize mistakes and sweep past any failures as quickly as possible because lingering there could damage precious self-esteem. Continue to strive and seek your own personal version of happiness because all the answers you ever need are already inside of you. If this formula rings even partially true, then humility indeed looks like an old-fashioned virtue, culturally irrelevant, and certainly not very useful to leaders today.

However, the type of humility that has been found to have a powerful impact at the very highest levels of leadership does not equate to meekness or display itself as mere modesty. For our purposes, humility can be defined as "a willingness to accept the self's limits and its place in the grand scheme of things, accompanied by low levels of self-preoccupation."[vi] This definition emphasizes both deep self-awareness and the broader ability to understand the big picture. The most effective leaders in the knowledge economy embrace a modern brand of humility that understands that it is literally impossible to have all the answers. Instead of having to be the smartest person in the room, a humble leader creates space for everyone to contribute and adopts a collaborative leadership style engaging all levels of the organization. A humble leader agrees with C. S. Lewis's notion that "humility isn't thinking less of yourself, but rather thinking of yourself less" and knows that pride is best focused on organizational rather than individual success.

While we may naturally resign leaders of a humbler stripe to a bygone era, I would insist that humility is extremely relevant and desperately needed for leaders today. The best leaders are those who possess the ability to display both great confidence and persuasiveness but also remain open-minded and curious. We will also see that humility is not the opposite of ambition, but rather it channels ambition to the greater good. Lastly, I will show how humility creates a formidable advantage by protecting leaders from the poisons of arrogance and hubris. These are the tragic, self-inflicted wounds that regularly fell even the smartest and most successful.

If we return to the questions asked at the beginning of the chapter, we must acknowledge that our initial instinct may be to gravitate toward the impressive charisma of Executive A. Hank Greenberg was the prototypical Executive A. Yet he lacked a critical ingredient that cost him dearly. Over the course of time, Hank Greenberg became grossly overconfident and displayed a callous arrogance. He took great pride in being "recognized as the smartest, canniest, and most successful insurance executive in the world" and reportedly relished the fact that he regularly made the Forbes listing of the "Ten Toughest Bosses." When federal regulators looking into his increasingly complex transactions challenged him, his standard reply became, "You just don't understand insurance."[vii] It is important to understand that Greenberg was actually forced out of his position as CEO in late 2005—nearly three years before the crisis of 2008. He was forced to resign by his handpicked board because the New York attorney general, Elliott Spitzer, uncovered aggressive accounting practices resulting in overstated earnings exceeding nearly $2 billion. Greenberg considered this error "immaterial" and fought to stay in control of the company. When questioned directly about the regulatory issue during an earnings call in 2005, Greenberg commented they were turning "foot faults into murder charges."[viii]

Could a strong dose of humility really have saved the world economy from near collapse in 2008? The question is interesting and infinitely complex, but if there is even a chance that the values and leadership style of Executive B could prevent similar future issues, then we owe it to ourselves to seek the answers.

Chapter 2

DON'T FEED THE EGO

A leader isn't worth his salt if he isn't willing to help set up chairs.
—Unknown

The average Fortune 500 CEO makes $10–$12 million per year and is surrounded by virtually unlimited executive perks. They often control the fates of hundreds of thousands of employees' careers, and shareholders depend heavily on their business savvy and good judgment. However, statistics demonstrate that our most prominent business leaders don't last very long. Despite their generous perks and pay, the average Fortune 500 CEO lasts only 4.6 years—a little more than a single presidential term.

At the other end of the scale, we know small business owners still create the majority of new jobs in the United States. However, data still indicates that close to 80 percent of small businesses fail within the first eighteen months. With millions spent each year on scouting and vetting top talent, it may surprise you to know that from 2003 to 2013, quarterbacks drafted in the first round of the NFL draft failed at a 50 percent rate.[ix] In business, politics, and sports, our top leaders fail at an alarmingly high rate with disastrous downstream consequences for their organizations and communities. While competition is exceedingly intense in these positions and burnout rates may always be high, do we not have a right to expect better, more consistent leadership from those at the top?

DUSTING OFF HUMILITY

In the previous chapter, we learned how the little value of humility suffers from a modern-day image problem. Millions of books are sold every year with the implied promise to help leaders "break through" and become even more successful. These self-help books offer better ways to innovate or execute, or focus on the new hot topic—qualities like executive presence, grit, or resilience. I enjoy these books and have found many extremely useful throughout my career. Yet, at the writing of this manuscript, I was surprised to discover that there was only one major commercial publisher to *ever* publish a book with "humility" in the title (*Leading with Humility* by Jeffrey Krames, 2014). Unfortunately, egomaniacal corporate executives cannot be sent to humility-awareness training. Nor are there any Humility 101 courses offered in the country's top MBA programs. However, recent research from some influential circles is beginning to shed light on why this is such a problem, and humility is slowly emerging as a critical success factor for contemporary leaders.

In 2014 and 2015, Google was named the number-one place to work by Glassdoor.com. This site is considered highly credible because it asks current and former employees to rate their company's culture and benefits while offering the cover of anonymity. Because of their reputation as an innovative technology company, most would assume Google hires people based on their IQ and technical skill sets. Laszlo Bock, the former senior vice president of people operations for Google, freely admits that high intelligence is somewhat of a prerequisite at Google, but he is quick to point out that something more is required. "The number-one thing we look for is general cognitive ability, but it's not IQ. It's learning ability. It's the ability to process on the fly. It's the ability to pull together disparate bits of information."[x] He links this learning ability with the process of learning from failure and talks about how Google is often wary of hiring newly minted MBAs who appear to have a sparkling record of success. "Successful bright people rarely experience failure, and so they don't learn how to learn from that failure." Block correctly reasons that Google's highly competitive environment may not be the ideal place for individuals to experience that first taste of failure. Block is certainly not the first Silicon Valley executive to recognize the usefulness of failure. However, his interview with Glassdoor caused a minor stir on the blogosphere when he spoke openly about humility as one the top five qualities Google looks for when selecting new employees. He explained that the best employees have the ability to step forward and demonstrate initiative but that they also need "the humility to step back and embrace the better ideas of others."

Thomas Malone and his team of MIT researchers have conducted extensive studies of small group dynamics to try to understand what types of teams are especially adept at creative problem solving—the type that is especially critical at innovative companies like Google. Their research found that the most creative groups—those that surfaced more and better solutions—shared three key qualities. First, they gave one another roughly equal time to talk. They shared the floor and had a roughly equal exchange of ideas. Second, they scored high on social sensitivity. The individual team members were more tuned in to one another, to subtle shifts in mood and demeanor, and displayed empathy for each other's perspective. Lastly, the most successful groups contained more women. While this last finding generated the most notice in the popular press, what they didn't find was equally as powerful. Their research showed that the most successful teams were not made up of the smartest individuals or the team with the highest collective IQ. But rather those that were able to step in and also step back appropriately to allow the best solutions to emerge. As Block correctly stated, "without humility, you cannot learn," and the teams that were best able to tap into their collective intelligence were able to arrive at the best solutions.

While appreciation of humility may be slowly gaining traction in Silicon Valley, there is even more evidence that a lack of humility amongst powerful leaders can have disastrous effects. With an energetic frock of white hair reminiscent of Albert Einstein, Professor Stanley Silverman at the University of Akron has spent years cataloging the detrimental effects of arrogance in the workplace. Silverman defines arrogance as a pattern of behavior that demeans others in an attempt to prove competence and superiority. Arrogance can be particularly damaging in team-based organizations because there is a social dimension to it that means I must tear someone else down in order to build myself up. It is essentially schoolyard bullying, and yet it continues unabated in many of today's biggest companies. Through years of research, Dr. Silverman has found that not only do arrogant leaders failure more spectacularly, they also have lower overall cognitive ability and regularly demoralize their peers and direct reports. People have long suspected that over-the-top arrogance may actually be a cover for deeper inadequacies, but Silverman's research is some of the first to prove it. The jerk who felt like they had to knock everybody down a peg and ran off all the best performers was in fact covering for their own lack of skill or knowledge.

Not only did Silverman's research bring to light the lower intelligence of more arrogant leaders, but he also teamed up with colleagues at Michigan State University to develop a practical instrument to help identify leaders that may struggle with arrogance. The Workplace Arrogance Scale (WARS) is a series of questions that can be incorporated into a typical 360 review. Silverman believes arrogance is "less a personality trait than a series of behaviors," which he believes can be addressed through coaching if the arrogant individual is willing to listen. Most importantly, his research points to humility as the antidote to arrogance and stresses that cultivating humility among leaders promotes a positive learning orientation and leads to more overall workplace productivity.

MIRROR, MIRROR ON THE WALL

While Dr. Silverman has been making a convincing case against arrogant managers, many of his colleagues have begun to demonstrate the negative effects of narcissistic CEOs who consider themselves corporate celebrities and seek to polish their personal brand on the backs of their shareholders. If arrogance is a team sport, narcissism is classically defined as excessive self-love or self-absorption. In other words, all you need is a mirror. In one of the foremost studies on narcissism in CEOs, Don Hambrick of Penn State University found that more narcissistic CEOs spent more on advertising (as a percentage of sales), spent more on R&D, ran up higher costs, and took on more debt. The more narcissistic CEOs tended to do more acquisitions and pay much higher premiums for the companies they bought. They also found that narcissistic CEOs produce large boom-or-bust cycles and that often performance would fall off dramatically after they left. A recent study conducted by the business schools at the USC and Arizona examined the impact of CEO narcissism on corporate tax policies. They found that corporations with the most narcissistic CEOs seem to be prone to engaging in highly risky corporate tax-avoidance maneuvers.

For a narcissist, every person, situation, or event is simply a platform to reflect his or her glory or a threatening chance to lose prestige. Protecting their ego and burnishing their image is priority number one—consequences be damned. Intelligent and astute at political maneuvering, a narcissistic leader can often fool others into thinking he or she shares in the larger mission of an organization. However, eventually there will be a situation where the narcissistic leader is asked to sacrifice, to choose the well-being of the organization over themselves, and in that moment, their true character is most clearly revealed.

HOW TO STUDY HUMILITY

When Don Hambrick first began his research on the effects of narcissism on CEOs, he ran into a problem. While he had a short list of CEOs within the tech industry he wanted to interview, he wasn't having any luck getting past their various corporate gatekeepers. It wasn't that he had a poor reputation as a researcher; in fact, he found many potential targets very friendly upon his initial call. However, when he explained the topic of his research, the reception often turned icy. It seems most CEOs were not flattered they had been targeted for a study on narcissism. In fact, he had such bad luck with his initial approach he was forced to devise a very clever yet indirect method to conduct his research using only publicly available information.

He and his coauthor, Arijit Chatterjee, studied more than one hundred CEOs in the computer and software industries between 1992 and 2004, and they were able to come up with four key measures to define a CEO's relative level of narcissism. The four factors they indexed were:

- The prominence (size) of the CEO's photo in the annual report
- The number of mentions of the CEO in company press releases
- The CEO's use of "I" in public comments to shareholders
- The gap between the CEO pay and the pay of the second highest-paid executive

While I have already discussed the fascinating data their study produced, their methodology of how to study the personality traits of reluctant participants was without a doubt their original stroke of genius. In many ways, the challenge in studying humility is even greater.

When the CEOs targeted in Hambrick's narcissism research declined to participate, they were able to identify tangible evidence of narcissism available in the public record. Ironically, when it comes to humility, often the best evidence is a lack of evidence itself. If we were to try to reverse engineer Hambrick's study, we might be able to come up with some creative measures, but humility is a slippery trait to try to nail down in a research setting. Imagine if I walked into a room of Fortune 500 CEOs and announced that I was conducting research on the relationship of humility to success.

If I were to ask for the ten most humble executives to report to the front of the room, I would likely either find myself alone or with the wrong individuals. The paradox is that those who are truly the most humble would never claim to be. I have come to call this the humility-hypocrisy problem. The core problem being that any self-proclamation of humility invalidates the claim and invites charges of hypocrisy. More simply, bragging about being humble instantly reduces your credibility and may even cause others to question your intelligence. Perhaps if I asked for anonymous nominations from peers, we could get a better list of people to study, but again, truly humble leaders would likely resist the focus on themselves and make reluctant subjects for study.

Despite the inherent challenges, some intrepid social science researchers have begun to make headway, and the early returns are impressive. Professor Michael Johnson found in a 2012 study that humble employees make better leaders because they foster learning, which helps with employee retention and overall job satisfaction.[xi] Another recent study published in the *Academy of Management Journal* by Bradley Owens demonstrated that humble leaders can be more effective because they are able to more easily admit mistakes and model "teachability."[xii]

Beyond the boardroom, Don Davis and his colleagues have collaborated on some interesting research that indicates that humility can even improve your love life. In a series of three studies, they found strong evidence that humility facilitates "the initiation and maintenance of romantic relationships" and even improves your chance of success in maintaining a long-distance relationship.[xiii] The humility-hypocrisy problem is real, and future social science researchers have much left to do if they hope to statistically prove the value of humility for leaders. However, let's now turn our attention to the one researcher thus far who has been able to popularize the idea that humility—instead of being a detriment to great business leaders—is actually one of their defining features.

The Capstone Quality of Great Leaders

Perhaps the most well known research into the positive effects humility can have on leaders appears in Jim Collin's seminal work, *Good to Great*. In this best-selling book, Collins demonstrated that the very best leaders, what he called "Level 5 leaders," combine tremendous personal humility with intense professional will. Rather than lacking in fire and drive, these leaders have it in spades. The difference is that their ambition is tempered by humility and channeled toward the larger goals of the organization itself rather than the selfish needs of their ego.

Following Collin's paradigm, I have referred to humility as the capstone quality of leadership. Collins explains that leaders have to progress through a series of stages, starting their careers as capable individuals (Level 1), becoming solid contributors to a team (Level 2), and later learning to manage others (Level 3), before finally becoming effective leaders (Level 4). At the top of every pyramid is the capstone, and it represents the culmination of the structure. While it makes sense to think of the capstone as the crowing piece of the overall architectural structure, the secondary function of the capstone is actually that it protects the structure. It offers protection from the rain, wind, and erosion that naturally occurs over time. Similarly, I believe that a leader who progresses to the very top of his/her chosen profession faces enormous pressure and temptation from the types of disastrous leadership sins that occur at the top. Narcissism creeps in, hubris steadily distorts reality, and arrogance erodes the foundation. Abraham Lincoln stated that absolute power inherently corrupts, and therefore it is at the top that humility's protective power is needed most.

It is equally important to understand that genuine humility does not diminish other critical leadership qualities that we rightly associate with excellence in leadership. As Collins illustrates, these qualities are the foundations of great leadership. Indeed, leaders need to be confident, bold in the face of competition, and ambitious both for themselves and their organizations. However, humility is not the opposite of confidence, nor are humble leaders devoid of personal ambition. Narcissistic leaders use their leadership perch as a platform to display their own personal greatness. Over time the work becomes less and less important; it is the prestige of their positions and their celebrated reputations they fight to preserve. Arrogant leaders also do not plan for succession. After all, what better testament to your personal greatness than to see the place fall to pieces after you eventually exit? In both cases, humility is badly needed to combat these very common leadership excesses and make sure those in positions of power continue to serve for the right reasons.

Jim Collins claimed it was the paradoxical combination of "personal humility" and "professional will" that combined to distinguish Level 5 leaders. In seeking to understand what makes the very best leaders, I asked a follow-on question—which of these two qualities is harder to find? It seems we have many capable leaders that are exceedingly driven and possess the intense professional will required. Why do so few seem to have the personal humility? If we have a potential abundance of Level 4 leaders, how come so few are able to break through and move to the next level? It is a fascinating question for leaders to ponder. Just how rare are legitimate Level 5 leaders? And if humility is truly the missing ingredient, what can be done about it?

Chapter 3

REIMAGINING THE HUMBLE LEADER

The sufficiency of my merit is to know
that my merit is not sufficient.
—St. Augustine

On Thursday, April 2, 2015, *Time* magazine's reigning Man of the Year could be found down on his knees washing the feet of prisoners. The setting was a detention center located on the outskirts of Rome, where the featured guest arrived early to greet 150 of the 2,100 men and women held in the facility telling them, "I'll wash the feet of twelve of your brothers and sisters who represent all of you here today." As he gently wiped the foot of a female inmate, she silently wept as he dried her foot and then stooped to kiss it. The assembled crowd was hushed, except for the shutter click of high-speed lenses from a nearby photographer. In speaking to the assembled crowd, he urged them to pray for him asking that the Lord would "wash away my filth that I may become more your slave."

Back in 2013, *Fortune* magazine began putting out an annual list of the world's fifty greatest leaders. They intended to cast a wide net, including elected government officials, CEOs, chiefs of NGOs, coaches, athletes, artists, and more. While they claimed it was "not enough to be brilliant, admirable, or even supremely powerful," their list of qualifying characteristics was in many ways very familiar. The profile required leaders with "vision," "effectiveness," and the "courage to pioneer." No doubt if this list were compiled in 2005, Hank Greenberg would have been a shoe-in.

However tried the methodology, the initial list garnered significant attention primarily because of who they placed in the number-one position. The selected individual was not a titan of industry, nor the most fashionable trendsetter. They didn't select the politician with the best comeback story or the hottest young artist. They didn't try to make the designation into a career achievement award for sustained excellence. Surprisingly, they selected a geriatric, newcomer to the world stage who had been on the job less than a year. Perhaps most shocking, they selected a religious leader named Jose Bergolio, better known as Pope Francis, as the number-one leader in the world.

LEADING FROM THE KNEES

Pope Francis's ancient, symbolic act of service demonstrates the stark power of humility when wielded by an esteemed leader. However, the ritual itself did not originate with Pope Francis. The previous year, Pope Francis visited an elder care center known as Don Gnocchi where he gently and patiently washed the feet of the chosen dozen—many of whom were in wheelchairs due to feet swollen and disfigured by disease. The sacred ceremony originated with Jesus Christ himself washing the feet of his disciples before the last supper, but it became an official part of the Holy Thursday service in 1955 when Pope Pius XII inserted it into the mass. However, this tremendous gesture of humility and service unexpectedly became hollow over time. Previous popes would carry out the foot-washing ritual on Holy Thursday in Rome's grand St. John Lateran basilica, and the twelve people chosen for the ritual would always be ordained priests. Some popes barely managed to get their hands wet in following a sacred tradition that they clearly found distasteful. However, Pope Francis, leader of what some had dubbed the "gentle revolution,"[xiv] was trying to shake things up. He wanted to challenge the establishment, get people to think, and perhaps make some uncomfortable.

He did this not with brash talk or self-serving pronouncements but by an incredibly compelling act of genuine humility. He asked not for exalted clergy but for prisoners. He didn't ask for men; he bucked the traditionalists by specifically requesting that women be included (which had never been done before). He even included two non-Christians. The message he sent was powerful. This new pope was here to serve, not be served—with authenticity, with genuine compassion, and with a spirit of humility that recognized the powerful impact that the laying down of power can have on people desperate to believe in their leaders once again.

POPE OF FORTUNE

We have established that the traditional leadership narrative is often flawed and that a lack of humility can be extremely risky for leaders. Which then begs the question, where can we look to find leaders of a different stripe? Where are the leaders who combine confidence and humility in just the right balance? Who are extremely driven and extremely successful but do not fall victim to arrogance or become entangled by excessive pride? Leaders who are resolute and decisive but do not see themselves as infallible?

It turns out that *Fortune* wasn't the only member of the popular press praising the leadership style and cultural transformation the new pontiff had been able to engender in such a short period of time. In 2013, Pope Francis surprisingly received an award from *Forbes* magazine for Disruptive Innovation. He was later named *Time*'s Person of the Year at the end of 2013. The new pope became such a cultural phenomenon that he truly broke new ground by appearing on the cover of *Rolling Stone* in January 2014. All this begs the question—what was it about Pope Francis that made him newsworthy enough for *Time*, successful enough for *Forbes* and *Fortune*, and cool enough for *Rolling Stone*?

THE GENTLE REVOLUTION

From the start of his elevation, Pope Francis has chosen one simple word to describe both his personal leadership style and attitude he wishes to engender in within the church— humility. He is not just paying lip service to the concept, as it has imbued his actions ever since the first day he assumed his most elevated position. It is tradition within the Vatican for the pope to don the historic regalia, including the famously tall and ornate hats, and provide a blessing over the faithful crowds gathered in St. Peter's square. Instead, dressed in a simple white tunic, Pope Francis first asked if the crowd would pray for him as he assumed office. Instead of a more traditional name, he chose to adopt the name Francis in honor of the saint known historically for his simplicity, poverty, and love of nature. Eschewing the trappings of a celebrity, he got rid of the pope-mobile (for a modest Ford Focus) and lives at a Vatican guesthouse rather than surrounding himself in the opulence of the pope's traditional palace.

His words have also reflected an unusual level of candor and self-critique as Pope Francis tried to shift the church's culture from one of institutional self-preservation back to its core mission of serving society's most vulnerable. According to tradition, the pope is seen as the direct successor to St. Peter and even viewed as the mouthpiece of God on earth. In fact, the doctrine of papal infallibility declares that the pope can be preserved from the possibility of error and can declare infallible doctrines. Yet, in this unique position of absolute power and prestige, the pope has instead demonstrated restraint, patience, and modesty. While his role gives him the power to judge the sinful from the righteous, he has instead asked how he can serve and heal. When asked about divisive cultural issues such as homosexual priests, Pope Francis humbly replied, "Who am I to judge?"

Through his consistent words and actions, Pope Francis has provided an initial glimpse into the transformative power of humility and created a radically different leadership template. He has been bold but also warm and charming. He has been resolute and harshly critical of those in power but also is willing to admit the limitations of his knowledge and ask for help from a wide circle of advisors. Perhaps most striking, in a position of nearly unlimited power and influence, he has opted for restraint and asked genuinely, how we can serve better?

In the introduction to their annual list of the world's top leaders, *Fortune*'s editors acknowledged that today's leadership isn't the same as yesterday's. Indeed, students of leadership too often fool themselves into thinking that all excellence in leadership requires is the creation of an extensive checklist of skills and behaviors that have proven valuable to leaders throughout history. Too often, context is ignored in favor of traditional ideas. Yet as the pace of change continues to accelerate, it is important to evolve and update our leadership formula to include the elements most critical today. The editors of *Fortune* nailed it when they declared, "Successful leadership may be eternal, but it's also brand-new." I firmly believe that humility has reemerged as a crucial element for successful leaders and will demonstrate why I believe that this quality provides a distinct and sustainable advantage for both individual leaders and their broader organizations.

THE HUMILITY ADVANTAGE

It is now time to change the conversation and create a new profile for leadership in the twenty-first century. It is time to recognize the critical value and importance of humility to the success of leaders. And it is long past time to disavow the notion that humility equates to weakness or timidity. For far too long, we have put up with the outdated notions of the charismatic leader who achieves positive short-term results but drips with arrogance, alienates colleagues, and inevitably combusts in a dramatic fashion. It is also time to reject the excuse that poor interpersonal behaviors are allowable because leaders achieve great results. That success cannot be obtained without extremely personal ambition, excessive pride, and even questionable ethics. These are leadership lies that must be put to rest.

Today the conversation has begun to shift. It starts with recognizing humility as a vital characteristic to becoming an extraordinary leader. Rather than a disqualifier for leadership, it should be an unequivocal requirement. This means humility is something we should actively seek out and select when considering top leadership positions. In this chapter, I will make the case that humility creates a distinct and sustainable advantage for leaders and for their organizations. This advantage is created for four fundamental reasons:

1) **People want to work for humble leaders**. This isn't about being liked; it is not that humble leaders are necessarily kinder or gentler. This is about what humble leaders do differently to inspire and drive employee engagement and long-term loyalty. In nearly every industry, there is an ongoing war for top talent, and humble leaders are best positioned to win.

2) **Humble leaders are more effective at leading change**. In a world where the pace of change is accelerating daily, successful leaders must be masters of change. I will demonstrate why humble leaders do this best.

3) **Humble leaders outperform ego-driven leaders**. Rather than thinking that humility places some sort of natural cap on how successful a leader can be, I will argue that humble leaders simply outperform more ego-driven leaders when measured against standard industry financial metrics.

4) **Humble leaders better position the organization for long-term success**. Lastly, humble leaders have a unique mind-set that enables them to see beyond short-term thinking and enable sustained success.

WHO DO YOU WANT TO WORK FOR?

Rather than rely on heavy-handed position power or fear to drive performance, one of the hallmarks of a humble leader is that he or she is approachable. They spend time with their employees and within the organization to get better information and drive collaborative decision making. Being approachable can take on many forms. It means keeping an open door, genuinely listening when employees share their ideas, and never insisting that you are too busy for your direct reports. As Lazlo Block at Google stated, approachable leaders "create space" within the organization allowing diverse opinions to come forward resulting in better overall decision making. It doesn't do any good to hire the best people and then just tell them to follow orders. Leaders who demand simple obedience and insist their ideas must always win out quickly find their most talented employees will disappear.

At the heart of approachability is an unwillingness to lazily rely on the power of your position to force people into compliance. Being approachable also means a leader is humble enough to generously share their most valuable asset—their time. Research into employee engagement from the Gallup organization has demonstrated that employees whose managers hold regular meetings with them are almost three times as likely to be engaged as employees whose managers do not hold regular meetings with them.[xv] Gallup also found engagement is highest among employees who have some form of daily communication with their managers (whether face-to-face, phone, or digital). Among employees who strongly agree that they can approach their manager with any type of question, 54 percent are engaged. When employees strongly disagree that their managers are approachable, 98 percent are disengaged. When you are the boss, a natural barrier exists between you and your employees. Being approachable means actively working to break down this barrier, driving deeper engagement and allowing you to get the very best out of your people.

One of the most powerful ways for leaders to actively model humility is to be vulnerable enough to admit mistakes. A humble leader doesn't have to appear to have all the answers. They are comfortable not being the smartest person in the room. They don't feel threatened when team members challenge them or offer a diverse perspective. They have the ability to step back and let a better idea emerge as their team engages in creative conflict. Best-selling author Patrick Lencioni passionately believes the best teams are built on what he calls "vulnerability-based trust."[xvi] In his book *The Advantage*, Lencioni says, "At the heart of this vulnerability lies the willingness of people to abandon their *pride* and their fear—to sacrifice their *ego* for the collective good of the team." This means admitting when you were wrong, speaking freely when you disagree, and being comfortable saying things like "I need help." Lencioni admits this type of vulnerability is uncomfortable at first. In fact, he likens it to "getting naked" in front of your coworkers, a concept that many leaders find threatening.

The idea of openly baring your flaws in a competitive professional environment is not something many people are initially excited about. However, Lencioni insists it is exactly this ability to be genuine and put forward your authentic self that creates a powerful connection among teams. Over time, this develops into a deep sense of trust, which becomes liberating to the team and increases their overall effectiveness. They are freed to take risks and innovate, knowing they don't have to try to hide their weaknesses or watch their backs. In his work with hundreds of organizations, Lencioni has come to recognize the single most powerful thing a leader can do to help drive this type of trust is go first and offer his or her own story with candor and genuine vulnerability.

Many years ago, I had the honor of working within an organization with a highly respected CIO that modeled this type of humble leadership. One of her direct reports recalls a time when their executive leadership team was working on developing this type of trust and somebody worked up the gumption in a staff meeting to challenge the CIO. This person said, "One of the things we need more on this team is the ability to disagree and challenge each other openly. It seems like whenever we get into a heated discussion, you jump in to try and play the peacemaker rather than letting us hash things out." The CIO, to her credit, didn't take the bait and engage in a heated exchange. Instead, she paused for a moment and said, "You're right. The ability to challenge each other and engage in creative debate is something we need more of, and I probably do inhibit it at times." She then went on to tell the story of how she grew up with an alcoholic parent and that there was no shortage of loud and heated arguments in their household. She said over time one of the coping mechanisms she developed was to become very calm whenever heated exchanges broke out and to seek to deescalate the conflict. She admitted that while this served her well growing up, this instinct didn't always add value and that she would work on it going forward. You can probably imagine the collective response within the room. She completely disarmed them with her vulnerability and also simultaneously brought them closer as a team. This is the type of powerful effect humility and vulnerability can have within a team.

Long-term approachability and vulnerability combine to create a culture where employees are more engaged and more loyal to the organization as a whole. They feel understood, valued, and safe. Therefore they are more willing to experiment and take on risk. A myriad of HR data tells us highly engaged employees serve customers better and ultimately drive better organizational performance at the bottom line. But perhaps more importantly, we know highly engaged employees will put extra discretional effort into their work. They contribute with their hearts as well as their minds and will go above and beyond in pursuit of the organization's goals. Strong leaders recognize it is this freely given discretionary effort that makes all the difference in a competitive industry. It is not enough for people to just do what they are told and put in their mandatory forty hours each week. As a leader, you have to tap into something extra and convince people, at a deep level, that their additional sweat and strain is worth it.

A classic command-and-control leader thinks motivating employees is a simple matter of carrots and sticks. Dangle a carrot to incentivize the majority and then drive the reluctant with threats or force. If done well, a leader may be able to get 100 percent out of their employees, but the leader will never get 110 percent or even 101 percent. They will only do what they are paid to do. A humble leader, by contrast, will engender loyalty and inspire people to give that *little* bit of extra effort that can make all the difference. In the end, the choice becomes self-evident—all you have to do is ask yourself, "For whom would you want to work?"

ARE YOU CURIOUS?

One of the key characteristics of an effective leader is the ability to set a new direction and guide people through the difficult transition process of getting there. Leaders must be masters of change, and humble leaders have a distinct advantage when it comes to this critical leadership task. But what makes humble leaders more effective in leading change?

In his book *The Corner Office*, Adam Bryant tells us one of the key defining characteristics of the very best CEOs is that they are "passionately curious."[xvii] They are always learning, always taking on new information. They solicit diverse opinions, even from their critics and those outside their industry, so they can continue to improve and change ahead of their competitors. Contrast this approach with arrogant leaders who believe they know best and love to have people coming to them to seek their wisdom. The ability to stay curious when you have reached the top is what distinguishes humble leaders from their competitors. Which begs the questions, why is it so difficult to remain curious?

Within any large organization, one of the risks for leaders as they are successful and move up the traditional hierarchy is they get further and further away from the front lines. This means they don't hear directly from customers anymore and may begin to lose touch with their employees doing the hands-on work. Whatever information they do get is filtered through layers of management who apply the appropriate level of spin to the original data. If given a choice, the vast majority of employees would rather present their boss with positive information. Well-intentioned employees may also seek to provide information that backs up their leader's opinions rather than present data that contradicts the goals originally set forth. This attempt to insulate their leaders from reality ultimately creates a distorted view of what is really going on in the marketplace or with their customers.

If a leader tends toward arrogance, this problem can be exacerbated because they may intentionally surround themselves with people who avoid challenging them. In the most extreme example, US presidents notoriously fall victim to this isolation phenomenon after several years in office. Sequestered by their Secret Service agents and the deferential treatment they receive from nearly everyone they encounter, the president can become grossly out of touch with the realities that normal everyday Americans face—often comically so. During the 1992 election, incumbent president George H.W. Bush suffered a major decline in the polls when he was caught at a grocery store checkout line and was clearly mystified by the apparently "new" electronic barcode scanner. It had been so long since he went to the grocery store he was hopelessly out of touch, and it came back to hurt him significantly when running against a young, fresh-faced populist named Bill Clinton.

The ability to stay curious and to embrace continuous learning is at the heart of what world-renowned Stanford University psychologist Carol Dweck has called the "growth mindset."[xviii] Dweck contents there are essentially two kinds of people in the world—those with a growth mind-set and those with a fixed mind-set. People with a fixed mind-set believe their basic qualities, like their intelligence or talent, are fixed traits. They have a certain amount, and that's that. This often means their goal becomes simply to look smart or at least never look stupid in front of others. They believe talent alone creates success, and essentially the world becomes myopically viewed as a battle between the haves and the have-nots.

In contrast, those who embrace a growth mind-set believe their most basic abilities can be developed through practice and hard work. They don't deny talent and genetics play a large role but rather view those as starting points. Those with a growth mind-set strongly believe through hard work they can accomplish things of great significance. This view then creates a passion for continuous learning and self-development. Adherents to the growth mind-set embrace Stephen Covey's maxim to continuously "sharpen the saw," and Dweck believes that virtually all great leaders—whether in business, sports, or politics—are distinguished by this growth mind-set.

This concept of the growth mind-set is very compelling. The notion we can improve our lives through education and training is as old as the Enlightenment, and the ability to improve one's circumstances through hard work and persistence is the very essence of the American dream. However, if it is really that simple, then why doesn't everyone embrace the growth mind-set?

BEWARE THE GURUS

Humble leaders make learning a priority and encourage others to do the same. They do so, not because it makes for a good HR slogan or helps in recruitment of employees, but because they recognize that the reality of globalization means innovation continues at a breakneck speed across almost all competitive industries. The pace of disruptive change has turned the idea of a long-term competitive advantage into an oxymoron. Google recognized this when they rated the ability to learn as the number-one factor they look for in new hires. They don't value knowledge of existing practices so much as they want employees who can learn fast enough to begin to shape new industries that don't yet exist. Given the nature of the information economy, Peter Drucker declared that teaching people how to learn was the most pressing task for all managers. He famously hated the designation "guru," which suggests that someone has become the recognized authority in his or her particular domain. Instead, he suggested leaders should always cast themselves as students who are constantly open to new ways of thinking. Adhering to this principle, every year Drucker assigned himself a topic about which he knew nothing and made it the subject of intense study.

Continuous learning is absolutely critical because rapid change and disruptive innovation are truly the only constant force in business today. Those who have confidence not in their knowledge or past experience but rather in their ability to work hard possess the humility to be successful in a future that is being created daily. It is impossible to have a growth mind-set, to embrace continuous learning, without a foundation of intellectual humility. Intellectual humility means honestly assessing what you do know but always being aware that there are things you do not know. A humble leader is naturally more comfortable with the ambiguity and uncertainty that always accompanies change. They do not cling to past patterns of success and are able to display a calm and genuine confidence when leading others through change.

Truly groundbreaking changes require people to do things they have never done before. Stepping out beyond the limits of their knowledge or expertise requires courage because it means they will likely make mistakes. The ability to acknowledge this fact and continue moving forward, despite any trepidation, requires a balance of confidence and humility that can be difficult to summon. It is much easier to remain safely within the security of the known and comfortable. But the disruptive nature of change forces us to realize that this security is a temporary illusion. If we embrace this realization, then our strength is no longer found in static knowledge but rather within the curiosity and the continuous desire to learn and grow. This is the solid foundation of confidence that a humble leader operates from, and we will see in the next section how it leads to peak performance.

HOW THE HUMBLE OUTPERFORM THE PROUD

In chapter 2, I credited Jim Collins and his team as being responsible for being the first to really popularize the notion that humility is an important ingredient for contemporary leaders. However, at this point it is worth taking a deeper dive into his research to underline the most important point his team discovered as they sought to understand what separates the good from the great.

In the beginning of their comprehensive research process, Collins established the specific criteria they were going to study. They were looking at Fortune 500 companies across all industries that outperformed the general stock market by three times. This constituted "great" financial performance. They also felt that being great shouldn't be a temporary blip. They quickly agreed that a sustained performance should stretch out over a fifteen-year period. After starting with these well-defined criteria, Collins and his team jumped into what he described as a "six-month death march of financial analysis" that examined at every Fortune 500 company from 1965 to 1995. They were looking for the mystical and inspiring essence of greatness within a sea of statistics and financial data. Yet Collins soon became frustrated with his team and the data they were producing.

In trying to understand what made a company great, Collins admittedly had a distinct bias. He didn't believe in quarterback syndrome. The basic theory of quarterback syndrome is this—the quarterback is the most important position on the football team, and therefore if the team is successful, they must have a great quarterback. The opposite is also true. If your favorite team stinks, then it must be because the quarterback is a loser as well. Collins felt this notion overly simplistic and in fact told his team explicitly to avoid the easy explanation that may tempt them to credit the leader or alternatively to blame the leader. He wanted answers based in scientific fact and repeatedly pushed his team to look deeper and even to "ignore the executives!" However, as his team did their research, they began to push back. They argued that all the data indicated there *was* something unique about the executives, and they couldn't simply be ignored.

As the team pushed further with their inquiry, they interviewed the executives and asked them to rank the top five factors in their company's transformation from good to great. To Collins's simmering ire, one annoying concept kept coming up. The executives kept mentioning the very unscientific concept of luck. The executives at the companies that became great often credited their success to being lucky. To provide a better contrast, Collins's team also studied and interviewed a team of comparison leaders who ran similar businesses in similar industries. When they would question these leaders about why their companies didn't perform as well, they would ironically also blame luck. They were just on the wrong side of it. The mentions of luck were so persistent that the team came up with a principle called "the window and the mirror" to capture what set apart the great executives from their peers. The principle states, "Level 5 leaders look outside the window to apportion credit to factors outside themselves when things go well. At the same time, they look in the mirror to apportion responsibility, never blaming luck when things go poorly."

As we saw in chapter 2, intangible concepts like humility are often very difficult to pin down or to subject to statistical modeling. Collins and his team repeatedly had to overcome their own bias to acknowledge the power of unscientific explanations such as luck. However, three key facts stand out from his research that cannot be ignored. The first is simply that leadership is critical in making a company great. Collins's team affirmed this notion even when they initially started with a bias against it. Second, they uniquely identified Level 5 leaders as being distinguished by their personal humility. Putting these two key factors together reveals that humble leaders explicitly outperform other leaders given the same set of circumstances and are more, not less, successful in producing results. Remember that the Level 5 leaders highlighted by Collins outperformed the market by three times. They didn't do just a little bit better; they *crushed* their better-known competitors (although they would never say so!). It is also worth recalling that Collins's research only identified eleven companies over a thirty-year period that could measure up to this standard of greatness.

If the executives studied won't brag for themselves, then somebody needs to in order to get across the larger point. We need to kill, once and for all, the flawed idea that humility is a hindrance for leaders. That a humble mind-set somehow holds them back or prevents them from being successful. Humility does not equal meekness any more than arrogance equates to strength. Humility should be clearly recognized as a defining strength of great leaders, one that creates a discernable advantage for themselves and their organizations.

For centuries, we have intuitively known that leadership matters. But our idea of what makes great leaders has ignored the crucial element that Collins and his team identified. Collins describes Level 5 leaders as a study in duality. Given his great insights into the importance of humility, we will explore what lies on the other side of this duality and how the best leaders use both parts of their nature to achieve a balance that can truly change the world.

Chapter 4

THE SUCCESS PROBLEM

After crosses and losses men grow humbler and wiser.
—Benjamin Franklin

COULD HUMILITY SAVE YOUR LIFE?

From a very young age, Laurence Gonzales had an obsession with survival. As a ten-year-old boy growing up in the baby boom era, he would occasionally accompany his father to his job at the Houston Medical Center where he served as a research scientist. While he often found his father's science experiments dull, he was fascinated by his reputation as a courageous, swashbuckling pilot. His father was a first lieutenant for the Eighth Air Force toward the end of World War II. In the last year of the war, he was designated as the lead plane on a bombing run over central Germany, and just as they began their run, his B-17 was mortally wounded by antiaircraft fire. With their wing severed at 27,000 feet, the aircraft began a terrifying inverted spin. In all the commotion, his father somehow managed to secure a parachute. Miraculously, a local German peasant discovered him lying in an open field. He was unconscious and gravely injured but alive. His crew was not so lucky. Of the ten-man team that began the bomb run, he was the only survivor.

Growing up on tales of his father's death-defying survival, Gonzales sought to prove his own courage, becoming a pilot at a young age. Later in his professional career as a journalist, he found himself drawn to writing about tales of survival against great odds. As he combed through the details of hundreds of accident reports and wrote dozens of articles, he began to wonder about the mysterious boundary between life and death. He wanted to discover what made the difference when a person found themselves in extraordinary circumstances that required split-second decision making with everything on the line. He began to ask why, given nearly identical situations, one person may live and another may die. He also dove into the science of survival, examining what makes the difference for high-risk professionals, including Navy Seals, smokejumpers, and NASA astronauts. Was it a matter of proper training and preparation or simply just blind luck? How could we rationally explain why an experienced hunter might perish while lost in the woods for a single night, whereas a four-year-old child may survive?

Gonzales's initial research revealed that only 10 to 20 percent of people have the ability to stay calm and think in midst of a survival emergency.[xix] To study how fear moves in with lightning speed to cloud our decision making and rob us of the critical ability to think clearly, Gonzales spent time with US fighter pilots on the enormous aircraft carrier *Carl Vinson*. He wanted to know what it takes to land an F-18 Hornet on a moving ship in the middle of a moonless night. It turns out that despite their rigorous preparation and training, most of the pilots admitted that fear was a major factor. As Gonzales explains, "The first rule is: face reality. Good survivors aren't immune to fear. They know what is happening, and it doesn't scare the living shit out of them. It's all a question of what you do next." The pilots knew fear was a very real part of the equation, so it became more of a question of how to make fear useful. One of the pilots explained how a good pilot is able to harness that raw fear: "Fear puts me in my place. It gives me the humility to see things as they are." These pilots understood that fear is a normal and undeniable reality in extreme situations. However, if they accepted that fear, they were able to channel it usefully to keep themselves sharp and, in many cases, alive.

In a contrasting example, Gonzales tells the tragic story of an army ranger, Captain James Gabba, who drowned on a guided commercial rafting trip down the upper Gauley River in West Virginia. Confident and healthy at thirty-six years old, Gabba was well trained to survive when he was thrown from his raft. However, when a guide acted quickly and attempted to provide him with assistance, he reportedly just laughed and pushed him away. His behavior, while puzzling, didn't necessarily mean he had a death wish. Rather Gonzales intimates the problem was much simpler. He surmised that as a well-trained army ranger, he probably felt like he was not in any real danger, rather, "He must have felt good, too, masterful, confident." He didn't have the healthy fear necessary to grasp the situation as it was and understand that, despite his pervious training, he was in dire peril.

Through studying these real-life examples of life-and-death situations, Gonzales came to pinpoint humility as playing a critical role in survival situations. However, it is deeper than just a casual reminder to remain humble in the face of nature. Gonzales draws inspiration from Zen philosophy indicating that in survival situations, a closed attitude, an attitude that says, "I already know," may cause you to miss important information. Zen teaches openness. Survival instructors refer to this quality of openness as humility. He further explains, elite performers—who risk their lives to save others—such as rescue professionals or astronauts, "have an exceptional balance of boldness and humility." They have to be simultaneously bold and decisive, retaining the ability to act but also cognizant of their natural fear to remain humble and perceive the situation accurately. Unfortunately, this balance is exceptionally difficult to maintain, thus the reason we are drawn to heroic figures who seem to have the right stuff and are able survive in the most extreme circumstances.

However, too often when trying to understand what the right stuff entails, we put the emphasis on the boldness and neglect the important role of humility within elite performers. The former is easier to capture in vivid colors and put on a Hollywood movie screen, whereas the humility inspired by healthy fear is much harder to portray and appreciate. We must remember that it is the interplay and balance between these two important qualities that creates a successful outcome. To let one crowd out the other is what causes catastrophe. In the next section, we will look at why this balance is so hard to maintain and why a successful outcome may ironically be the most dangerous outcome of all for our long-term success.

HOW SUCCESS LEADS US ASTRAY

In previous chapters, we have reviewed how humility can be a critical factor in making leaders more effective and thus more successful. However, what if success itself becomes a barrier in allowing us to tap into the power of humility? If you spend time reading the biographies of great leaders, you will often see how humility seemed to come upon them as a result of a dramatic failure or setback. In *The Road to Character*, David Brooks closely studied the lives of many legendary historical figures, from Saint Augustine to General Eisenhower, and came to the conclusion, "There is one pattern that recurs: They had to go down to go up. They had to descend into the valley of humility to climb to the heights of character." He further explains, "In the valley of humility they learned to quiet the self. Only by quieting the self could they see the world clearly." If we accept this premise, then a type of twisted, circular logic presents itself. Humility is necessary for success. However, the only way to obtain humility is through the crucible of failure—which by definition is the opposite of success. The equation doesn't seem to add up. Faced with this confusing proposition, many people may reason that the cost of humility is simply too high.

We will come back to these hard questions, but first let's take a step back and examine the relationship between confidence and success to see how it might aid in answering our larger questions.

If we go back to the standard profile of the charismatic leader, we will find one of their defining characteristics is their high level of confidence. Admittedly, we prefer leaders who lead with a powerful confidence born of success. Confidence can be very contagious within organizations. We naturally look to leaders and expect them to be bold in standing up for our organization or moving against tough competition. Leadership ranks simply do not seem to be a place for bashful, shrinking violets that lack self-confidence.

This makes logical sense because there is a natural relationship between success and confidence. Whether we are learning to write complex code, master a new language, or snow ski for the first time, a familiar pattern emerges. In the beginning of taking on a new task, our confidence is lacking or very low. After all, this is something new, and as a novice, we have no track record to fall back on. However, if we have the courage to forge ahead and begin, we start to make progress. It may be slight at first, but as we struggle and strain to learn the new skill, through a process of trial and error we improve. As we improve, however slightly, we cross a threshold of achievement and experience some small measure of success. If we keep working and begin to stack up successive achievements, our confidence grows proportionally. Successful achievement breeds confidence, and a virtuous cycle emerges whereby this newfound confidence encourages us to keep going and push past our previous limits, thus achieving greater success.

Admittedly, we should expect this virtuous cycle of progress to be punctuated by dips in achievement or failures. When we fail, our confidence retreats. If we demonstrate the necessary grit and resilience to push forward, however, the symbiotic march of confidence and success continues on an upward trajectory. This back-and-forth cycle where success breeds confidence, and greater confidence informs success, is fundamentally how we learn. However, at some point success can become a bad teacher.

When exploring this topic in the corporate leadership classes, I often ask those present, "How successful do you want to be?" Or, "On a scale of one to ten, tell me how much success you would like to have in your life." Most often I will get an honest answer of ten or perhaps an ambitious "Eleven!" While success is inherently subjective and comes in many forms, most achievement-oriented leaders agree—if given the choice, they would not like to see their success capped or place any artificial limit on what they can achieve. It has been humorously said that there is no such thing as too much money or too much fun, and it seems too much success may also fall into this categorization. We tend to think of success as an unlimited good. However, when we begin to ask the same questions with regards to confidence, a different picture emerges.

If there is no natural upper limit on success, confidence is a quality that at a certain point offers diminishing marginal returns. As previously acknowledged, confidence does indeed serve us well, especially for those in leadership roles. It projects optimism and signals competence and passion to those we lead, and it inspires them to follow. It feeds upon success and serves us very well—up to a point. The problem is there comes a time when healthy confidence crosses a thin line and quickly erodes into overconfidence. Overconfidence is dangerous because it makes us believe we are smarter than we really are. It encourages us to take further risks or to continue doing what we have previously done, even though the situation may have changed. Being overconfident creates a form of situational blindness that skews our perception of reality, thereby making us susceptible to disastrous errors in judgment. Overconfidence can also alienate those around us and evolve further into the toxic stew of arrogance and hubris we learned about in chapter 3.

The dangers of overconfidence are real, and the temptation to cross this thin line is strong for even the best leaders. Returning to *Mindset*, Carol Dweck chose to highlight a powerful anecdote that served as a formative moment in the career of Jack Welch, the revered CEO of General Electric. She explains how early on in his career, Welch was criticized for being arrogant and told he didn't take critical feedback well. During a period of great success in his career, he made several successful acquisitions and felt like he could do no wrong.

Then he bought Kidder, Peabody, a Wall Street investment banking firm with an Enron-type culture. It was a disaster that lost hundreds of millions dollars for GE. "The Kidder experience never left me." It taught me that "there's only a razor's edge between self-confidence and hubris. This time hubris won and taught me a lesson I would never forget."

Welch's story underscores just how thin the line between healthy self-confidence and destructive overconfidence can be. In reality, it is exceedingly easy to cross this line, even if unintentionally, and once we do cross it, it is extremely difficult to backtrack and save ourselves. Normally the only cure is a punch in the gut from reality, signaling unequivocally that we have caused our own demise. It is a bitter pill to stomach.

For a time, we may even continue to gain further success even while displaying ever more reckless forms of overconfidence. However, in the end, the illusion is always shattered. Unfortunately, when overconfidence and arrogance have propped up a leader far longer than a healthy situation would dictate, we witness some of the largest and most significant failures. Writing for *Forbes* magazine, Eric Johnson effectively articulates the trap that so many leaders fall into. "Optimism is healthy. Arrogance is not. Self-confidence is healthy. Megalomania is not. Believing that you can do a great job as CEO is healthy. Thinking that you know better than others is not. You need confidence and conviction to succeed as a CEO or in life, but what these studies clearly show is that—taken to extremes—narcissism kills companies and kills CEO careers."[xx] Because the powerful interplay between success and confidence is so seductive, he even manages to empathize with leaders that find themselves snared. "I can understand why many CEOs go too far in their self-confidence. Throughout their whole careers, they've been rewarded for taking risks and showing self-confidence. It's like they keep betting on red and winning 11 times in a row. What are you going to do on the 12th time? Bet red and be more confident than ever."

Leadership expert Marshall Goldsmith refers to top executives who display this tendency to cross the line into overconfidence as "success junkies" in his book *What Got You Here Won't Get You There*.[xxi] His best seller is based upon the sharp insight that there is a fundamental paradox of success. He would agree with Johnson's contention that, "successful people have very few reasons to change their behavior." He intimately understands the virtuous cycle of success breeding confidence and how this positive reinforcement is extremely hard to counteract without self-awareness and disciplined action. Goldsmith believes top leaders are seldom brought down by a lack of skill or intelligence but rather self-destructive interpersonal behaviors. Number one on his list of these destructive behaviors is the need for competitive leaders to "win at all costs and in all situations—when it matters, when it doesn't and when it's totally beside the point." While a competitive drive to win is important in achieving success, this drive and confidence can turn on you and actually become destructive to your long-term growth. When confidence becomes overconfidence, a long-win streak can quickly transform into a crushing defeat.

MAPPING YOUR CONFIDENCE

This overconfidence problem poses many difficult questions leaders must be aware of and struggle with. When does healthy confidence, bred by success, become overconfidence? How can I tell as a leader if I am close to crossing the thin line where I become susceptible to the dangers of success—including arrogance, hubris, and narcissism? Because effective self-diagnosis is inherently difficult, I encourage leaders to spend some time in an exercise of self-reflection on their careers to explore some of these difficult questions. Here's how it works:

First, I instruct them to take a basic piece of graphing paper and label the y-axis as confidence. Along the x-axis, they are instructed to plot time, measured in years. To provide enough of a sample size, I normally ask them to explore a ten-year period of their career and chart their relative level of confidence over that ten-year period. This starts with identifying career milestones that easily come to mind. A significant promotion, a new product launch, or perhaps when they met an influential mentor. Normally this type of event results in a rise in confidence due to the virtuous cycle we discussed previously. Of course, not all milestones are positive, so participants should also include key mistakes or failures as well. These normally include losing a key account, being reorganized into a different division, or being laid off due to changing economic conditions. As participants begin to log their unique career history on paper, most begin to chart a rising and falling pattern that resembles an EKG with its familiar peaks and valleys.

Now that they have a recent career map, the real work begins. The first step is to recognize some common features of the terrain:

- **Wins:** A sharp rise in confidence is appropriately labeled a "win"—this is when your career surged ahead with a great assignment, a promotion, or some other tangible feeling of success. These are the good times characterized by lots of momentum and expanding opportunities. During these times, we feel validated, get to be a part of a great team, or perhaps receive various types of recognition or rewards.
- **Dips:** Alternatively, there are the easily recognizable dips on our map. These are times when we experience a drop off in confidence due to our own mistakes or failures. These are the scary moments when our plans go off track or are destroyed completely. They are characterized by stress, turmoil, and feelings of loss.
- **Plateaus:** We also experience periods of relatively flat advancement that can often last for a long time. We label these plateaus. These are the times of slow advancement—normally our confidence will continue to advance as we get more comfortable in a role, but success does not always match the pace. We may also get stuck and find ourselves limited, whether artificially or not. Depending upon the

circumstances, these can be either times of steady, patient growth or frustrating times of stagnation.

After we have mapped out the basic terrain and understand the features, I ask participants to engage in some critical self-analysis. Can they find any patterns that emerge to perhaps help them see their own history with new eyes? First, they are instructed to make a note of any sharp changes in direction. What typically happens after a sharp rise? What about after a dip?

Next, I ask them to consider the thin line where confidence deteriorates into overconfidence. Looking back on their careers, can they recognize any times when they may have crossed that line and become overconfident or even fallen into arrogance? If so, what was the result? They can also begin to explore broad, more overarching questions. When do you tend to be most effective? Where in your career did you learn the most? What can you do to avoid the very real pain you felt in your deepest dip?

It is through this type of honest personal analysis the real power of humility emerges. When applied against the patterns of our own lives, we can see humility has three very powerful benefits. They include:

- **Prevention of self-inflicted wounds**. Arrogance can cause us to miss important information, and hubris can distract us from the real business at hand. Humility helps to counteract this situational blindness and thereby can prevent some mistakes from ever happening. Humility serves as a kind of antidote to combat our natural tendency toward overconfidence. It protects us from this destructive and frustrating self-sabotage that reoccurs so often for many leaders. When provided a position of power, humble leaders do not become entrapped by the prestige of their position or fall into destructive self-absorption.

- **Extending a win**. Although humility alone cannot prevent all dips or keep you winning forever, it can keep you sharp and provide the accurate perception needed to allow you to continue to improve even in the midst of success.

- **Improved resilience.** Humility doesn't make a mistake any less painful. But it does allow a humble leader to more easily acknowledge their role, study the mistake, learn from it, and move on. It can make a dip shorter and less severe. Failure doesn't feel fatal or permanent to a truly humble leader, so they rebound quicker and ultimately grow stronger from their mistakes.

In this chapter, we have explored the complicated relationship between confidence and humility. I have attempted to demonstrate that humility is not the opposite of confidence but rather a powerful agent to prevent confidence from turning toxic.

Oxygen is fundamental to life, just as confidence is to leadership. But too much oxygen can become dangerous. The primary gas in Earth's atmosphere is not oxygen; it is actually nitrogen at 78 percent, followed by oxygen at about 20 percent. The phenomenon of oxygen toxicity or oxygen poisoning is a major concern for underwater divers or those on high concentrations of supplemental oxygen. If too much oxygen is consumed, a condition known as hyperoxia can result from an excess of oxygen in body tissues. The side effects include disorientation, breathing problems, vision changes, and in extreme cases death.

Just as oxygen toxicity can be deadly, overconfidence and arrogance damage more careers than anything else. Hopefully I have driven home the point that we don't have to make a false choice between confidence and humility. You need both to be a great leader. Overconfidence has a range of nasty effects and continues to ensnare unsuspecting leaders, resulting in severe damage to reputations and careers. The truly scary part is that while a career downturn is terrifying for an individual leader, it is often even worse for the organization. In the next chapter, we will turn our attention from the individual to the organization and explore if humility has power to transform organizational cultures and prevent the common turmoil we see in many companies today.

DO YOU KNOW WHERE YOU ARE?

In *Deep Survival*, Gonzales includes a fascinating chapter entitled "Bending the Map" that explores the psychological processes of people who become lost in the wilderness. He starts with Professor Edward Cornell's research, revealing, "that being lost is a universal human condition." But despite its ubiquity, there is actually a "very fuzzy area between lost and not lost." Gonzales explains in great detail how our brains are wired to make mental maps of our environment, and fundamentally, what we call "being lost" is simply a mismatch between our mental map and the actual environment. He goes on to point out how in the midst of our daily lives, most "people operate on the necessary illusion that they know where they are. However, most of the time, they don't."

Similarly, I have observed that most leaders become lost at some point in their careers. In climbing the corporate ladder or in the midst of striking out into new territory, their mental map and their actual environment become mismatched. However, out of ignorance or fear, few are willing to admit it. Gonzales also tells us that psychologists who study the behavior of people who get lost report that very few ever backtrack. Those lost in the actual wilderness often have the necessary equipment to survive. They may even know the way back, but the fear and panic associated with the mental state of being lost clouds their judgment and sets off a terrifying chain of events.

If you are a leader, the thin line between healthy confidence and destructive overconfidence should be a concern. Despite our general sense that we know where we are it is very easy to lose perception. It is easy for our mental map to become bent. This is why humility has become absolutely imperative for twenty-first-century leadership. It is imperative to admit the limits of our perception and acknowledge we too can become lost. We must do better to ensure we do not become the next terrifying statistic of well-intentioned leaders who somehow lost their way and brought down once-healthy organizations. It is our responsibility to do better. To lead with the humility that gives us a fighting chance to stay on course and prevent future disasters from occurring.

Chapter 5

THE INSULAR ORGANIZATION

The fullest and best ears of corn hang lowest toward the ground.
—Bishop Reynolds

Insular is not a term we hear much these days. *Webster's* defines the word as "separated from other people or cultures: not knowing or interested in new or different ideas." The word was originally conceived to refer to island dwellers who were cut off from the outside world and therefore developed a narrow or provincial viewpoint focused only on their own immediate concerns. This extreme inward focus becomes all-encompassing, resulting in a general ignorance and even apathy to anything beyond the boundaries of our immediate vicinity and the people in it. We have already seen that an individual who is extremely self-absorbed will be described as a narcissist. However, we seldom describe individuals as insular. This is because an insular mind-set normally takes hold within a community of individuals. Insularity is a team sport that produces a dangerous brand of groupthink characterized by collective arrogance. Insularity is the organization equivalent of narcissism, and it comes with many of the same damaging side effects—only this time played out on a much broader scale.

Thus far we have focused on the ways in which humility can create a powerful advantage for individual leaders. The positive results of humble leadership for the broader organization have also been demonstrated, including improved financial performance, greater employee engagement, and long-term sustained success. In chapter 2, we learned about the grave damage the leadership sins of arrogance and narcissism can wreak on an individual leader's career. Now, it is worth examining what happens when these factors become ingrained in the culture of an organization. The result is best described as insularity, and the results are not pretty.

BP AND THE DEEPWATER HORIZON OIL SPILL

The morning of April 20, 2010 started ordinarily enough for Gordon Jones. The Louisiana State University graduate awoke early, grabbed a quick breakfast, and made a mental note to try to call his wife later that morning. The world's largest oil companies typically assign code names to offshore drilling sites early in the exploration effort, as this practice helps ensure secrecy during the confidential presale phase. Often the names stick and become convenient names for casual reference. Jones had been assigned to the "Macondo prospect" as a drilling fluids specialist for British Petroleum (BP). The oilrig was located about forty-one miles off the coast of Louisiana in the Gulf of Mexico. The name "Macondo" had been the winning entry from an internal BP United Way campaign a year earlier. It came from a fictitious, cursed town in the novel *One Hundred Years of Solitude* by Colombian Nobel Prize-winning writer Gabriel Garcia Marquez. Drilling the initial exploratory well with Tranocean's Deepwater Horizon unit began in early February and was proceeding on schedule. At the time, nobody had any reason to suspect that the operation would bear any resemblance to Marquez's notoriously hard-luck hamlet, but 5,000 feet below the surface, an epic disaster was about to unfold.

At around seven thirty that morning, BP vice president of drilling, Patrick O'Bryan, was on the platform to lead a small rally to celebrate seven years without a lost-time incident. He departed soon after leaving 126 crewmembers on board. Just before ten o'clock, the crew noticed the lights flicker followed by two noticeably strong vibrations. Moments later, a bubble of methane gas escaped from the well and shot up the drilling column, expanding quickly as it burst through several seals and barriers before exploding in a massive fireball. Amidst blaring sirens and fire alarms, terrified crew members began a chaotic evacuation as a spreading fireball engulfed nearly the entire platform. A total of 115 people would be evacuated with seventeen taken by helicopter to nearby trauma centers. After an exhaustive rescue effort that included two Coast Guard cutters, four helicopters, and a rescue plane, eleven crew members were declared dead, including twenty-eight-year-old Gordon Jones who left behind two young sons.

Despite the heroic evacuation that saved many lives, the environmental disaster was just beginning. Immediately after the explosion, officials estimated that the site was leaking approximately 8,000 barrels per day into the gulf. On April 22, two remotely operated underwater vehicles (ROVs) were sent down to attempt to cap the well but were repeatedly unsuccessful. All told, the sea-floor oil gusher would flow for eighty-seven days until it was capped on July 15, 2010. The incident would eventually be known as the largest marine oil spill in the history of the petroleum industry, nearly double the amount of oil spilled by the famous Exxon-Valdez tanker in 1989.[xxii]

PRIDE PRECEDES THE FALL

We have already demonstrated the power of success to lead astray even the finest of individuals into the well-laid traps of overconfidence and hubris. However, now we turn our attention to the organization as a whole to try to understand what broader effects result from arrogance at the top. Can the arrogance of an individual leader trickle down and permeate the ranks, creating an insular mind-set? Many companies strive to become the biggest or the best within their industry, but does reaching these goals create unique problems that must be considered? Finally, what role can humility play in counteracting these broader issues of organization health?

After showing us the proven formula to take an organization from good to great in his first book, Jim Collins and his team admittedly took a darker path in their third book as they became curious about the broad topic of organizational decline and failure. The result was a comprehensive case study in organizational disaster entitled *How the Mighty Fall.* Collins was initially intrigued by the fact that many precipitous declines seem to be self-inflicted, and the fall of large seemingly successful organizations can happen terrifyingly fast— almost as if it snuck up on unsuspecting leaders. With his unique talent to take large amounts of research data and condense it down into insightful models, Collins quickly came to see organizational decline as a five-stage process that begins with collective arrogance and ends tragically with either irrelevance or death.

Collins calls the first stage the "Hubris Born of Success" and notes this initial stage begins when a great company becomes "insulated by success." When a company is on a winning streak and has vanquished its closest competitors, it acquires a certain amount of momentum. This momentum can be powerful, and one of the insidious cultural side effects is what Collins characterizes as a "general shift from humility to arrogance." You can visibly see this whenever a company's marketing team starts to broadly boast they are the biggest, largest, or most successful within their industry. Once a company has reached the top of their industry, an attitude of entitlement can set in, and it can actually become difficult for a successful company to foresee how they wouldn't stay on top. Think about the market share that Blockbuster video enjoyed in 1996 (the year before Netflix came onto the scene) or how Radio Shack once dominated the consumer electronics industry. This collective overconfidence manifests itself in several ways.

Instead of keeping true to their core products or business units that produced their initial success, executives are prone to engage in a wide variety of interesting distractions. These include things like expensive new product lines, pursuing the synthetic growth of acquisition, or overreaching into difficult new markets. The financial stability produced by previous success effectively insulates the company from feeling the pain of this lack of discipline and sets them on the precipice of decline. This doesn't mean companies don't need to evolve and change. The pressure for growth demands it, and Collins is quick to point out that "great companies foster a productive tension between continuity and change," but those that experience long-term success never put their primary business on autopilot to purse flights of fancy.

The other key cultural indicator that emerges during this stage is a decline in learning orientation. This occurs when a company stops asking questions and starts answering them. Everyone wants to profile successful companies and find out their secret to success. However, it is precisely when a company thinks they have cracked the formula that their ability to learn is compromised. It is easy to become a media darling and spend time more time explaining your secret sauce than actually running your business. If the market is handsomely rewarding your company, it becomes tempting to believe you have all the answers. Collins points to Wal-Mart as a company that has bucked this trend and says that despite being the world's number-one retailer for years, their culture is one of "deep humility and learning orientation."

INSULARITY BEGINS AT THE TOP

The Horizon explosion and resulting oil spill were an epic disaster played out on CNN over the summer of 2010, but the failure of leadership was nearly as compelling. The annual report for 2009 reflected that BP logged record profits of just over $14 billion. Tony Hayward became CEO of BP in 2007. Hayward started his career as a field geologist and quickly rose through the ranks of the company's important Exploration and Production division, including a three-year stint as head of their operations in Venezuela. The door was opened for Hayward to claim the company's top position when previous CEO Jeff Chevalier perjured himself under oath to prevent his sexual orientation from becoming public and was forced to resign. When Hayward was named CEO in May 2007, the average price of crude oil hovered around a healthy $62 per barrel. Just over a year later, by July 2008, the price of crude would peak at $145 per barrel, massively increasing the fortunes of his company as well as Hayward's own personal net worth.

Looking back, it would be hard to find a global enterprise better positioned for success than BP in 2008. With the price of its core product at record levels and a young, talented CEO at the helm, it seemed they were poised for greatness. However, history has demonstrated that seeds of arrogance sown at the pinnacle of success become the critical determining factor between short and long-term success.

Speaking at a business school lecture in May 2009, Hayward spoke about key changes he felt needed to be made within BP. He stated bluntly that in the past BP "failed to recognize that it was an operating company" and lamented they had "too many people that were working to save the world." Hayward believed there were too many people who lost track of the fact that "their primary purpose in life is to create value for their shareholders." BP's safety record in years leading up to the spill would seem to reflect this renewed focus on operations and profits at the expense of environmental and employee safety. In the three years prior to the 2010 spill, the US Occupational Safety and Health Administration (OSHA) recorded hundreds of safety violations at BP's refineries, which led to a record-setting $87 million in fines. This shoddy track record during Hayward's tenure caused the US deputy assistant director of Labor for OSHA, Jordan Barra, to go so far as to claim that BP has "a systemic safety problem."

In the early days of the Deepwater Horizon crisis, Hayward initially attempted to downplay the spill, calling it "relatively tiny" compared with the "very big ocean." However, as the facts mounted, his denial quickly became hard to maintain. After six frustrating weeks, which included multiple failed attempts to stem the flow of oil into the gulf, Hayward attempted a public apology on May 31, expressing his sorrow to the American people for the disaster. Toward the end of his comments, he went off script and casually assured the reporters "nobody wants this thing fixed more than I do. I want my life back." The callous comment made professional crisis managers gasp and reflected the widespread belief that BP's leadership was dangerously out of touch. Hayward further reinforced this negative perception when he was photographed in June at a yacht race just two days after testifying before an angry US congressional delegation. The repeated faux pas would not be forgotten by thousands of angry residents along the gulf. Charlie Kronick of Greenpeace said Hayward was clearly "rubbing salt into the wounds" of people affected by the crisis.

What is interesting is that is wasn't always this way at BP. In his book *Crisis of Character—Building Corporate Reputation in the Age of Skepticism*, Peter Firestein tells of a time when BP's culture was quite different with a genuine focus on community collaboration and carefully understanding the environmental impacts of their projects.[xxiii] He cites the example of an ambitious effort BP undertook from 2003 to 2005 to build a thousand-mile pipeline extending from the Caspian Sea through three countries to the Mediterranean. At the time, it was the largest infrastructure project in the world and very important to the company's future growth. They understood no matter how big the project was to BP as a company, it would have even longer lasting effects on the communities they built through. The team at BP was proactive and conducted thousands of interviews with people along the proposed route to find the least disruptive path to minimize the impact on the environment. Although this approach cost valuable time, BP was determined to do it right, and in the end they were praised for setting new standards in corporate social responsibility.

The Horizon Deepwater spill was a disaster of epic proportions, and it is easy to look back in hindsight to recognize the mistakes BP made. However, it is harder to directly link an insular culture to specific actions. How did a company so focused on community collaboration and environmental impact in 2005 become a notorious repeat offender by 2010? We can certainly point to the change in leadership, as there is little doubt the attitude of leadership bears significant responsibility. The words and actions of leadership matter a great deal. They send signals to the organization about where priorities lie and what values they are to embrace. Perhaps even more important is where an organization chooses to spend their valuable discretionary capital. When oil prices crashed during the 2008 economic crisis, Hayward responded by slashing costs, including those for safety and environmental discovery efforts. There is no scientific instrument available to accurately measure the relative level of insularity within an organization, but there are warning signs and hallmarks of an insular culture that can cause us to further consider whether a company is focused on the right things:

1) **Secrecy.** A certain amount of discretion is always needed in business to protect trade secrets or valuable intellectual property, but some companies become obsessed with secrecy at the expense of healthy transparency. In *Crisis of Character*, Firestein recounts the story of when, "A very candid CEO once told me that the reason he insisted on transparency was to protect himself from himself, 'If everybody can see what I'm doing,' he told me, 'I'm less likely to do something stupid.'" Today, a good clue to a company's overall level of transparency is whether or not they embrace social media. If a company's leadership is not active on social media or actively discourages employees from using it with restrictive policies, this might be the sign of a larger issue.

2) **Concentration of power.** When CEOs serve within an echo chamber of agreeable lieutenants, the tendency toward groupthink becomes very real. A diverse leadership team and board members are needed to combat this tendency and reduce the chances of insularity creeping in over time. Access of employees to leadership is another strong signal. Do executives regularly engage with their organization or do they

spend their days jetting around in private planes and dining in an exclusive executive lunchroom?

3) **Employee disengagement**. If a company's bottom line looks healthy but their employee engagement scores are stagnating or in decline, this could be a sign of trouble yet to come. A multitude of data has established the link between high employee engagement and a healthy bottom line, but engagement scores are lagging indicators. It is often tempting for CEOs to engage in short-term behaviors such as downsizing or budget cuts that boost profitability but can also destroy morale over a longer timeline. Because most large organizations do not make their employee engagement scores public, this factor can be difficult to track from the outside, but the indicator is a useful marker of the relative level of insularity.

4) **Active resistance to oversight**. Any competitive global industry is likely subject to some form of governmental oversight or regulation. Healthcare, banking, and aviation are just a few critical industries that operate under heavy regulation. Individual organizations within those industries can differ greatly in their institutional response to oversight. Some will be proactive, establishing robust internal compliance functions dedicated to staying abreast and informed on regulatory changes. Others will adopt a defensive or even hostile posture with a strategy focused on defensive litigation or aggressive lobbying to attempt to fight any new forms of regulation. While some chaffing against regulatory pressures is normal within a free market, an actively hostile posture is a strong indicator of an insular culture.

5) **Lack of community involvement**. Most organizations profess an earnest desire to be active members of the local community in which they work, but this can also easily be lip service. Many companies are eager to publish the amount of money donated to various causes and enjoy sponsoring goodwill events to polish their brand within the community, and these

are certainly necessary and helpful. However, I would suggest that a truer indication of community involvement is actually the hours spent performing community service rather than dollars spent. If a company is willing to allow their employees time off the job for annual community service activity, this is an indicator of strong commitment and active, hands-on engagement.

The price tag for insularity is extremely high. When the failure is significant enough (the Horizon Deepwater disaster certainly qualifies), individual leaders may pay with their jobs, but the organizational damage is even longer lasting. On July 27, 2010, BP made the decision to fire Hayward and replaced him with Robert Dudley, the first American chief executive in BP's history. By then, the damage to BP's reputation and bottom line were staggering. In November 2012, BP and the United States Department of Justice settled federal criminal charges with BP pleading guilty to eleven counts of manslaughter, two misdemeanors, and a felony count of lying to Congress. BP would pay a record setting $4.5 billion in fines and was ordered to set up a trust fund to settle all criminal and civil penalties that would eventually cost the company a staggering $42.2 billion.

After leaving BP, Hayward admitted in an interview he "felt a bit lost," but nevertheless he seemed to enjoy his early retirement.[xxiv] Perhaps to clear his head, he engaged in a bit of adventure tourism, skiing in the French Alps and even scaling Mount Kilimanjaro. Still in his early fifties, Hayward quickly decided to reenter the oil business and took a risk by joining an emerging company called Genel Energy focused on extracting oil from the war-torn Kurdistan located in Northern Iraq. Although his new company was tiny when compared against BP, nearly two years later Hayward seemed to have learned a bit of humility, telling the *New York Times*, "I have been lucky. Having the opportunity to do something like this is fantastic. It is fair to say I wanted to recover some of my self-esteem."[xxv]

However, by 2015, Hayward was involved in an internal power

struggle with investors, and that led to his stepping down as chairman. Soon after, he tried to negotiate a sale of the company and find a replacement CEO to allow him to remain as chairman. Despite the struggles of his new company, it seems his ample confidence had been restored as he explained to the press that the move was not about his company but rather, "This is about my life, what I want to do. I'm 58 years old and I want a slightly less full-on life. I've done it for four-and-a-half years." Less than a year after making that pronouncement, the company's value plummeted more than 40 percent in one day after they were forced to downgrade the amount of oil they could pump from their core oil field in Kurdistan.

For many, the crucible of failure may teach deep and lasting humility, but for others it appears it is a difficult truth to master. Leaders that fail to learn from their mistakes, especially ones as public and disastrous as Hayward, are dangerous. Their personal arrogance and lack of humility breeds a collective insularity within their organizations. Because they are in charge, their own personal failings are amplified and pass on great risk to their extended network of stakeholders and customers. It is time to demand that leaders who are entrusted with great responsibility also have the necessary humility required of the position.

Chapter 6

HOW TO INCREASE IN HUMILITY

It is no great thing to be humble when you are brought low; but to be humble when you are praised is a great and rare achievement.
—St. Bernard (Italian bishop)

FACING DOWN FAME

The last football game Pat Tillman would ever play came against the Washington Redskins at FedEx field in Washington, DC, on January 6, 2002. Tillman's Cardinals took a 17–6 lead into halftime, but with under seven minutes left in the game, the Redskins got the ball back and began driving down the field, repeatedly pounding their 230-pound running back Stephen Davis into the heart of the defense. As the Redskins reached the red zone, Tillman made three consecutive tackles before Davis eventually overpowered the tired defense for a two-yard scoring plunge. The Cardinals failed to score on their last possession and lost 20–17, giving 61,721 shivering Redskins fans something to cheer about at the end of an otherwise uninspiring 8–8 campaign. Tillman, always a defensive menace, finished the game with nine tackles but did not speak to the media in the postgame locker room.

Although intelligent and articulate, Tillman, like most professional football players, did not particularly enjoy interacting with the media. The one occasion that last season when he did appear to open up was the week after 9/11 when he expressed his appreciation for his country and spoke of how easily things can be taken for granted. "You don't realize how great a life we have over here ... My great-grandfather was at Pearl Harbor and lot of my family has gone and fought in wars and I really haven't done a damn thing as far as laying myself on the line like that so I have a great deal of respect for those that have."[xxvi]

In his excellent biography of Tillman, *Where Men Win Glory,* Jon Krakauer recounts how Tillman went through an extensive searching process before sitting down at his computer on April 8, 2002 and typing up a carefully worded document entitled "Decision." It began simply stating, "Many decisions are made in our lifetime, most relatively insignificant while others life altering. Tonight's topic ... the latter." He then explained, "My life at this point is relatively easy. It is my belief that I could continue to play football for the next 7 or 8 years and create a very comfortable lifestyle for not only Marie & myself, but be afforded the luxury of helping out family and friends ... The coaches and players I work with treat me well and the environment has become familiar and pleasing. My job is challenging, enjoyable, and strokes my vanity enough to fool me into thinking it's important. This all aside from the fact that I only work 6 months a year ... For more reasons than I care to list, my job is remarkable ... In short, we have a great life with nothing to look forward to but more of the same."[xxvii]

Shortly after writing the "Decision," Tillman turned down a three-year $3.6 million contract extension from the Arizona Cardinals. Later that May, he informed the team's head coach, Dave McGinnis, about his plans to enlist in the army, and McGinnis questioned Pat about how he would address the intense media interest his decision would generate. The veteran coach realized that the NFL athlete-turned-soldier's story would be irresistible to the press. "You know," McGinnis told him, "this is going to cause a media storm. How are you going to handle it?" Tillman smiled, amused, and replied, "I'm not. You are." Pat thought his decision spoke for itself and did not want it to be perceived as a publicity stunt, so he told his coach he didn't plan on doing media interviews of any kind. True to his word, Pat and his brother Kevin enlisted at the Military Entrance Processing Station in Phoenix in June without uttering a single word to the press.

Dave McGinnis was proven correct. Once word of Tillman's decision became public, media outlets scrambled to contact Pat looking for an exclusive. Pat's agent, Tom Jones, recalls turning down over one hundred interview requests within the first week. Many people admired his decision to walk away from the NFL to serve in the army after 9/11; however, most were shocked even more by the fact that he refused to bask in the spotlight and receive the adulation he was due. *Time* magazine reporter Richard Lacayo commented on his modest refusal to cash in on his story, saying, "In a culture obsessed with money, there's something hard to believe about a person who turns down that kind of offer for an $18,000- a-year job with the Army. And in a culture obsessed with fame, we hardly know what to do with a guy who doesn't even capitalize on the story." From the minute he decided to sign up, Tillman refused interview requests. What he did wasn't a publicity stunt. It wasn't a career move. It was that ancient, compelling thing—a sacrifice."[xxviii]

Tillman's sacrifice was compelling on many levels. While turning down $3.6 million was headline grabbing, it was the more subtle and personal sacrifices Tillman spoke of in his decision that truly reveal his character. Pat opens by admitting his life is "relatively easy" and that his status as a professional athlete has afforded him the means to do what he wishes and also enrich the lives of his close family and friends. He also talks of how he enjoys his profession and continues to find it challenging. He is surrounded by talented teammates and coaches and has "nothing to look forward to but more of the same." In nearly every important way, Pat fit the stereotypical definition of what it meant to achieve career success. He had a lucrative job he found challenging, enjoyed the people he worked with, and was surrounded by a strong circle of family and friends. But the most striking line—the one that reveals the most—is when he wrote about how his status as a professional athlete "strokes my vanity enough to fool me into thinking it's important." This is powerful. In a society where everyone wants to be rich and famous, Pat Tillman was able to recognize this desire was pure ego and deny its basic premise. Even more than turning down money, Tillman did the unthinkable—he turned down fame and adulation. He recognized the hollowness of celebrity. Instead of allowing others to stroke his ego, he muzzled it by humbling himself to serve, not as an officer directing others but as a regular soldier putting himself in harm's way on the front lines.

Even after he penned his decision and informed his employer, he still fought resistance from within his own family. Understandably, they feared for his safety and begged him to reconsider. But Pat was not naïve or reckless; he knew this decision could be dangerous and would cause immediate pain for his family, especially his new bride of only two months. He ended his decision by stating, "However, it is not enough … I'm no longer satisfied with the path I have been taking … I'm not sure where this new direction will take my life though I am positive it will include its share of sacrifices and difficulty … Despite this, however, I am equally positive that this new direction will, in the end, make our lives fuller, richer, and more meaningful."

CAN HUMILITY BE LEARNED?

It is one thing to admire the humility in others but quite another to possess it ourselves. In fact, it is much easier to convince ourselves that people like Pat Tillman are uniquely rare—after all, who among us would willing give up what he did? While our sacrifice may never be of the same magnitude, I am convinced we must all eventually struggle with many of the same questions Pat did. What do you do when you recognize your environment has become "familiar and pleasing"? How do you handle it when success in a given area "strokes your vanity," giving you an overinflated sense of self-importance? What if you feel strongly compelled to move in a direction of greater service knowing that it will cause pain and hardship for your closest loved ones? These are tough questions with even tougher answers. However, I am firmly convinced humility can play a central role in providing these answers.

Up to this point, I have attempted to display both the intrinsic value and functional utility humility can provide in both personal and professional settings. However, the cost of humility is high, and at this point, an important question must be asked. Is humility something we are born with or something we are taught? Is it a mind-set that can be acquired with practice or something that may come to us over time? If I am convinced that humility is indeed worth pursuing, what can I possibly do to improve or increase my overall level of humility?

As we saw in chapter 5, humility can be difficult to find and even harder to hang onto. It is ephemeral, slipping away gradually or evaporating in plain sight as we move forward in life doing all the right things. But despite this elusive nature, a very practical question remains—where can I find humility and how can I keep it?

Fundamentally, there are really only two ways to learn something. We can learn directly from firsthand experience or indirectly learn through the related experiences of others. As newborns, we learned directly as we experienced the world with our five senses. We learned the sight of our parents and the sound of their voices. Spend two minutes with a toddler and you will quickly find that they will smell and taste anything they can get their hands on. Through the process of trial and error, babies learn that oatmeal is nourishing food and toy cars are not. Direct learning through our own experience is the most powerful way to learn, and we continue to learn this way throughout our lives. As the well-known truism declares, experience continues to be the very best teacher. However, there is a downside to this most direct form of learning. While it is certainly the most impactful, it is also the most labor intensive, expensive, and painful. It is also the slowest. The world simply has too much complexity and variety to experience everything firsthand.

From an early age, we also begin to learn indirectly from the experience of others. When your parents read you a book or told you a story, you indirectly learned from the hero's lesson. Later in school, students are taught the lessons of history and science. The first time you learned to cook, you likely followed directions to a recipe somebody else created. The advantage of learning secondhand is that you can consume the collective wisdom of generations that came before you relatively quickly. You may not be able to go whaling with Herman Melville, but you can read *Moby Dick* and understand a great deal about the process. You can't travel to Mars with the latest NASA rover, but you can watch YouTube videos to see and experience the faraway planet almost firsthand. While this type of learning is much faster and allows you to be exposed to the diversity and complexity of the universe, it is also acquired relatively cheaply and therefore isn't nearly as powerful. This is knowledge acquired by the head rather than the hands. One of my favorite movies is *Good Will Hunting*, and Robin Williams's character captures this difference beautifully when he tells Will, the young genius, that all his secondhand knowledge is superficial, safe, and unearned:

> So if I asked you about art, you'd probably give me the skinny on every art book ever written. Michelangelo, you know a lot about him. Life's work, political aspirations, him and the pope, sexual orientations, the whole works, right? But I'll bet you can't tell me what it smells like in the Sistine Chapel. You've never actually stood there and looked up at that beautiful ceiling; seen that. If I ask you about women, you'd probably give me a syllabus about your personal favorites. You may have even been laid a few times. But you can't tell me what it feels like to wake up next to a woman and feel truly happy. You're a tough kid. And I'd ask you about war, you'd probably throw Shakespeare at me, right, "once more unto the breach dear friends." But you've never been near one. You've never held your best friend's head in your lap, watch him gasp his last breath looking to you for help. I'd ask you about love, you'd probably quote me a sonnet. But you've never looked at a woman and been totally vulnerable. Known someone that

could level you with her eyes, feeling like God put an angel on earth just for you.

We continue to use a combination of direct, firsthand experience and a wealth of indirect knowledge to learn throughout our lives. The direct experiences are the most powerful and retained the longest, but we accumulate a treasured store of secondhand knowledge that also powerfully shapes our lives. As we consider how to learn about humility, it is worth considering which approach, direct or indirect learning, will be most effective. Said another way, it is one thing to know *how* to wash another person's feet and quite another to actually get down on your knees and start scrubbing.

When it comes to humility, a unique problem occurs as our most powerful firsthand experiences can actually work against us. If we work hard and apply ourselves, we begin to experience a measure of success. As a result, our confidence naturally grows unchecked, and over time, we get the feeling we can do no wrong. Our environmental stimulus (i.e., applause from an audience, a promotion at work, an award from the industry) teaches us that our way is always correct and reinforces it again and again. Until one day, blinded by pride and surrounded by well-meaning supporters, it can all come crashing down. Not surprisingly, we don't normally react well. After all, we have been betrayed by our hard-won firsthand experience.

You can read all about the utility of humility in chapters 1–5, but the most powerful way to learn the true nature of humility is to experience it in the depth of our own personal failures and mistakes. David Brook's contention that we must "descend into the valley of humility" can be a frightening harbinger for leaders currently experiencing the highs of success. Indeed, Admiral Stockdale similarly spoke of how all leaders require a course "in the familiarization of pain." But are pain, punishment, and the harsh sting of failure really required to gain the precious humility we seek? If we were being honest, most leaders would admit they actually go to great lengths to avoid these difficult lessons. If given a choice, what sane person chooses pain over pleasure, rejection over praise, and failure over success?

HUMILITY THIEVES

In trying to understand the best way to gain humility, it is also very useful to first pause and consider any external environmental factors that may conspire to gradually rob us of our humility. To simply blame the trapping of success is too generic and vague. We need to understand the key external influences that gradually move us in the wrong direction. We need to recognize and limit the factors that cause us to lose our humility. It starts with working to keep our perception clear during times of success and then responding appropriately to the unique obstacles it can bring. There is an old saying; it is easier to make it to the top than stay there. Here are some of the reasons why our humility is put at risk the minute we reach our goals:

- **Winning too much**. Those who love to compete often see winning as an unlimited good and can't get enough of it. Often this need to win extends far beyond their profession into civic events and even personal relationships. Fierce competitors feel the need to be out front in every situation, chair every subcommittee, and end every argument. When the scoreboard continually declares you the winner, it becomes ingrained in your identity, and it becomes hard to imagine any other alternative. The more the wins pile up, the easier it is for your humility to get lost in the shuffle.
- **Praise.** While the scoreboard may silently and satisfyingly reflect your glory, the accompanying praise and accolades that inevitably follow seem to shout from the rooftops. Writer Mathew Hutson has said, "Winning an award is about the least humbling thing in the world."[xxix] If you privately felt good about

your success before, then publicly winning recognition is an accelerant to the ego, burning up your humility in the process.

- **A supportive inner circle.** Often people who have experienced the ups and downs of success can learn not to fall victim to the media hype, but it is harder to resist the everyday backing of those closest to you. The reality is that those closest to you have the most to gain from your success and may occasionally withhold helpful criticism with the intention of being supportive. Are the people close to you strong enough to occasionally challenge you when you need it?

Success, awards, and a supportive inner circle—to most people this would encompass a pretty solid definition of what they strive for in life. It is certainly not something to be avoided. Admittedly, these are all positive, enjoyable, and mostly hard-won and well earned. However, when it comes to preserving and improving humility, these external factors are indeed threats. By recognizing the potential danger they bring, we can rightfully enjoy them in the short term without allowing them to sow the seeds of any long-term damage.

While these external factors are somewhat beyond our control, how we react to them is very much under our influence. Hall of Fame UCLA basketball coach John Wooden was famously quoted as saying, "Talent is God-given; be humble. Success if man-given; be grateful. Conceit is self-given; be careful." While we may not be able to avoid all external factors that erode our humility, recognizing how we process those external influences and understanding that conceit is indeed self-given can allow us a measure of control. This realization allows us to become proactive and take concrete action to avoid the loss of our humility. Here are a few actions we can take to begin to exert this control over the insidious influence of self-given conceit:

1) **Don't get too comfortable.** Beware the trappings of your position. When we have been in a leadership position for too long, it is easy to become entitled. To feel like we have done more, sacrificed more, sweated more and thereby we deserve

our office, title, or you-name-it executive perk. It happens slowly over time to well-intentioned leaders, but it still happens. Take action periodically to reexamine your relative level of comfort within your current position. Reevaluate any rewards you have earned over time and ask if they are in line with your peers and competitors. If not, be willing to relinquish them.

2) **Believing your positive press.** Those reporting from the outside seldom know how things really get done, so don't be taken in by the hype when times are good. This inflates the ego and robs you of humility. Pope Francis has been quoted saying that positive press is actually offensive and wasteful when there are much more newsworthy problems. Don't be so easily flattered. Don't spend time reading glowing press reports of yourself or your company.

3) **Don't surrounding yourself with "yes" people.** Guard against insularity by making sure you surround yourself with people who are not afraid to challenge you. Extend them trust and reward them when they bring forth difficult news or challenge your opinion. When hiring new people to your team, actively look for a diversity of styles and opinions rather than merely looking for individuals who see the world the way you do.

4) **Rationalizing mistakes.** By explaining away mistakes, you send the wrong message to your team, but you also miss the valuable chance to learn from your own mistakes and share them with others. Own your mistakes as much as your victories and be courageous enough to share them openly.

Is it possible for us to grasp the true nature of humility with secondhand knowledge? Can we achieve the positive benefits of approachability, curiosity, and a willingness to serve without personally plumbing the depths of failure? Or is the price of humility measured in our willingness to lose it all? My intent here is not to be dramatic or oversimplify this down to a binary choice but to illuminate the nature of how we learn and why humility is both hard to obtain and even harder to retain. We will return to these larger questions in chapter 8. For now let's address the very basic question of whether humility is a quality we are born with or something we can learn over time.

To help answer this question, we will return to the fixed mind-set versus growth mind-set that Carol Dweck introduced us to earlier. Those with a fixed mind-set would contend you are either humble or you are not. That Pope Francis was blessed with a humble spirit while Hank Greenburg will never understand it. While they may admit experiences can certainly inform the relative level of humility you display, those with a fixed mind-set fundamentally think there is not much you can do to become more humble.

In contrast, the proponents of the growth mind-set would view humility as a valuable character trait or mind-set that can be studied and improved upon with diligence and effort. Just as we can learn to be more patient, tolerant, or perceptive, increasing in humility is surely within our capabilities. Those who proscribe to the fixed mind-set may want to skip ahead to the next chapter. All others can continue reading to learn of specific actions you can take to continually and purposefully become more humble.

- **Embrace failure**. Initially, the idea of embracing failure seems counterintuitive. If you are reading this book, you were likely motivated to learn something that would make you a more effective leader. Your goal was to improve, to be more successful, and certainly not to fail. However, take a moment to acknowledge that maybe the only thing you have in common with the other readers of this book is that you have made mistakes in the past and will eventually do so again. To err is indeed very central to our human condition. The difference between a humble leader and an arrogant leader is what they do with those inevitable mistakes. Humble leaders own their mistakes, study them, and even share them with others. Humble leaders do not see failure as a threat to their ego or identity and ultimately get stronger and more resilient. Arrogant leaders rationalize mistakes, try to hide their failures, and as a consequence very often repeat them.

The group that has really mastered this concept of embracing failure is entrepreneurs. They use terms like "fail up" or "fail forward" to explain the iterative process whereby short-term failures ultimately guide them to success. They realize that in the pain of each stumble there is a natural opportunity to learn and redirect their next effort in a smarter fashion. In *Blackbox Thinking*, Matthew Syed powerfully illustrated how the aviation industry has hard-coded the idea of learning from failure into its processes and procedures so that deadly mistakes rarely reoccur.[xxx] On the opposite end of the spectrum, I have spent a good portion of my career in the health care industry, and unfortunately there is a widespread culture that is not very tolerant of mistakes and often stigmatizes failure. In his TED Talk from 2011, physician Brian Goldman speaks forcefully about confronting medicine's culture of denial (and shame) that keeps doctors from ever talking about their mistakes. Because failure is viewed so negatively within health care, Goldman sponsors an anonymous podcast each week allowing physicians to openly discuss errors and offer solutions to colleagues who may run across similar situations. Entrepreneurs and aviators are bold in their acknowledgment of error and sincere in their passion to eradicate it. Physicians unfortunately are often reluctant to admit error and even less likely to publicize it for fear of lawsuits or shaming by fellow colleagues. We increase in humility when we are comfortable enough to admit our own error and courageous enough to share it to benefit others.

- **Do something painful.** Humility requires the willingness to leave your comfort zone. We all need to remember what it feels like to be the new kid. To try something awkward or uncomfortable. Many high achievers spend their careers building specialized expertise and honing their craft in an attempt to achieve superior knowledge and reap the associated rewards. However, after reaching the pinnacle, many lose their edge and become stagnant or arrogant. It takes extreme self-awareness and personal discipline to step down and force yourself into a situation where you are inexperienced, unprepared, or not in control. When is the last time you started at the bottom or tried something outside your comfort zone? Are you occasionally willing to admit ignorance and take on the posture of a student or do you only operate in areas where you are the authority? We have seen humility often retreats with increasing expertise and is rediscovered in our ignorance and pain. But you don't necessarily have to experience this pain at work to reap the benefits. Travel to somewhere where you don't speak the language. Take on a new home improvement project or volunteer at a local hospice. Anything that gets you out of your comfort zone trims the ego and can provide greater perspective, thus improving your foundational humility.

A great example of a successful individual stepping out of their comfort zone was when Michael Jordan chose to walk away from the NBA to pursue a lifelong dream of playing professional baseball. Jordan was known to be one of the most competitive basketball players of all time and he admittedly had a healthy ego. His willingness to voluntarily relinquish his position at the very pinnacle of his sport to become a Minor League benchwarmer was quizzical to most. After all, we so rarely see those in positions of power or prestige walk away to pursue deeper self-learning. Most would not say they are purposefully seeking humility per se, but they would likely acknowledge it will be a natural part of the process, and they walk toward it with open eyes and open hearts.

- **Deflect praise.** As a leader, when you have achieved some measure of success, accolades will come your way. At that point, you have a fundamental choice to make. You can absorb praise or deflect it. Absorbing praise feels good—it strokes our ego and feels justified as a reward for our hard work. However, absorbing praise and listening closely to those who applaud you is probably the quickest way to erode your humility. Accolades should be for your team to help celebrate success and acknowledge their contributions, not for leaders to bask in the limelight. By deflecting praise to your team, you receive the benefit of improving your team's confidence and loyalty, but you also protect yourself from the damaging effects of arrogance and hubris.

The task of deflecting praise sounds relatively simple, yet the seductive lure of awards and acknowledgment are hard to resist. Here's an interesting experiment. The next time you visit the office of a successful executive or colleague, try to make a mental count of all the plaques, trophies, or certificates of accomplishment you see. These could be framed law degrees, philanthropic awards, or gleaming Lucite sculptures for various industry accomplishments. If you truly begin to take notice, you will see they are nearly ubiquitous. To counter this, I have challenged leaders to keep such items to a minimum and instead keep a failure board displayed in their office. This could be a bulletin board or whiteboard where they list the things that haven't gone to plan or were outright failures. Keep it prominently displayed where anyone may see it. Not only can a visual reminder keep you sharp, but it also provides a chance for others to ask you about your mistakes and creates natural teaching opportunities. High-performing leaders sometimes make mistakes, but few are fatal. Even critical mistakes can be more easily forgiven if openly admitted and explained in a way that signals they will not happen again. Have the courage to admit your mistakes, learn from them, and even share them in the appropriate context.

- **Commit to service.** To state it bluntly, you make a very poor leader if you only serve yourself. Promisingly, the tenets of servant leadership continue to gain traction within leadership circles, and savvy leaders are becoming more aware of how important it is to find new ways to serve their team members. This does not mean being submissive. After all, you are still the boss, but at a very basic level your team needs to know you care about them and are willing to work for and with them.

- **Plan to make yourself expendable.** No matter how high you rise and how successful you are, remember the graveyards are literally filled with indispensable people. Nobody is truly indispensable. A leader without a succession plan is like a husband with a wife and five kids and no will. It is selfish. Most leaders readily acknowledge the reality of the hit-by-a-bus scenario. The idea being that despite your overall importance to the organization, anyone could easily step off a curb tomorrow at the wrong time and get hit by a bus. It is a bit morbid but an effective idea that reflects a very stark reality. As talented, effective, and important you are to your organization today—you could easily be gone tomorrow. Even forcing ourselves to entertain such a scenario allows humility to seep into our thinking. Yet while many begrudgingly admit the real possibility of such a scenario, more often than not, we lead like it doesn't apply to us. If you haven't done it yet, make it a goal to put together a succession plan. It is an act of incredible professional maturity. It is a visible demonstration of humility and the acknowledgment that your time is limited and you are not indispensable.

ADOPTING A POSTURE OF HUMILITY

In her famous TED Talk originally delivered back in 2012,[xxxi] Harvard researcher and author Amy Cuddy introduced us to the surprising idea that we can change other people's perceptions, and even our own body chemistry, simply by changing body positions. We have always intuitively understood that how we feel about ourselves can readily manifest itself in our external body language, but Cuddy flips this notion on its head. Her research introduced the concept that power posing or standing in a posture of confidence, even when you don't feel confident, can actually affect your brain chemistry by increasing hormones such as testosterone and cortisol. This profound insight has no doubt forever changed how people prepare for job interviews. In fact, I suspect that if you were to wander into the restroom of a Fortune 500 company on any given day, you would be likely to find a well-dressed millennial standing in front of the mirror looking as if they were Clark Kent just coming out of a phone booth.

Cuddy's work reminds us that our body language and nonverbal behaviors have a powerful effect—not just on those we interact with but, most importantly, on ourselves. She demonstrates these poses are a universal language. They transcend culture and language barriers, and Cuddy has even worked out taxonomy to categorize and name certain positions. For example, the position she calls "pride" consists of arms outstretched to the heavens, eyes gazing upwards. Think of a sprinter at the Olympics who has just vanquished his top competitors and won the hundred-meter dash. The idea of power posing for two minutes to create a short-term but very real boost in confidence is very seductive. However, be careful. Follow-on research has also revealed people who assume high-power poses were also more likely to steal money, cheat on a test, and commit traffic violations in a driving simulation.[xxxii]

I have to admit I find Cuddy's research fascinating, which has led me to wonder if body language can also make us more humble. Think for a minute. What pose would you imagine communicates humility? I bet if I were to ask one hundred different people this question, it would come down to one basic pose. Getting down on both knees, arms at your side, head bowed to the ground. Whether bowing before God or the queen, I suspect this pose is also universal and can also have a dramatic effect on brains and our lives if adopted regularly.

For centuries, getting down on your knees has been a position of supplication, literally of lowering oneself before another. Our modern-day empowerment culture tells us that to kneel is to give away your power. The hero of the Mexican Revolution, Emiliano Zapata, famously said, "I would rather die on my feet than live on my knees." This is the powerful, independent spirit all revolutions seek to tap into. Many leaders sweat and strain their entire career to achieve a position of power that signifies they no longer are subservient to anyone. Once it has been gained, few are willing to set it aside lightly.

However, we have also seen there is very real power in humility. That voluntarily lowering oneself does not necessarily diminish power. In fact, I believe only those who understand power most intimately have the tremendous courage required to know when to set it aside. The message sent is undeniable. It has a leveling effect that connects the entire organization. It demonstrates healthy restraint and credibility of character. It can also be incredibly inspirational and generate genuine goodwill. The celebrity serving meals at the soup kitchen does not give up their fame any more than the pontiff washing feet gives up his elevated office.

Cynics may say that such symbolic gestures can be easily manipulated, but I would argue that it only makes the authentic examples all the more powerful. Displays of true humility by those in power can literally change the world. This is why the example of Pat Tillman continues to speak to us even if he would not. The challenge to the leaders of today is not only to wield power judiciously but also to know when laying power down can actually be the best use of it.

What if the simple act of getting down on our knees regularly could open our minds, provide perspective, and powerfully protect that which we have already earned? In the next chapter, we will explore the critical distinction between getting down on your knees and being brought to your knees. The distinction is small but critical, and understanding this crucial distinction can make all the difference in the world.

Chapter 7

SEEK HUMILITY OR BE HUMBLED

Everyone I meet is in some way my superior.
—William Shakespeare

NO HUMILITY AWARDS

I have always enjoyed teaching leadership development classes. I mostly teach for corporate audiences as part of company-sponsored development programs or high-potential leadership classes. In fact, this book actually began as a two-hour class I originally entitled "The Humility Advantage." As I get toward the end of this class, I like to bring up a slide showing a certificate of achievement. On the certificate it says, "Congratulations!" in big bold letters, and I ask the participants to give themselves a round of applause as a reward for completing the humility class. I let them know they can now tell their friends they are certified experts in humility. Normally, I get a few awkward smiles, maybe a nervous chuckle or two, before the on-screen certificate is crumpled up and falls off the screen. Apparently a two-hour course on the importance of humility for leaders does not leave people feeling like they qualify as experts, and that is probably for the best. Humility is slippery, and the moment when we become satisfied with our relative level of humility, it can begin to slip away.

In the previous chapter, we discussed the fleeting nature of humility and how it can gradually dissipate over time even if we are diligent and well intentioned. It is critical to realize that humility is not a destination. It is not a mountaintop you can arrive at, take a selfie, and move on. It is truly a journey, a lifetime discipline of character that must be persistently cultivated and pursued. It is very often a struggle between the person we are and the person we want to be. There are no quick and easy shortcuts to humility. Bill Wilson, one of the original founders of the Alcoholics Anonymous movement, knows a thing or two about struggle, discipline, and battling to maintain humility. In his book *Best of Bill: Reflections on Faith, Fear, Honesty, Humility, and Love*, he asks readers to consider the notion that obtaining perfect humility is probably impossible. Instead he urges them to understand how the act of continuous striving can actually be their redemption. "There can be no absolute humility for us as humans. At best we can only glimpse the meaning and splendor of such a perfect ideal."[xxxiii] As flawed human beings, he says the best we can hope for is to "seek humility for today."

Persistence, daily striving, and continuous seeking are a tall order for anyone. Diets seem impossible to maintain, our credit cards continue to pile up debt, and we still can't seem to make it to church every Sunday. If there is anything consistent within human nature, it is our consistent ability to fall off the wagon. The pursuit of humility requires us to battle this fragility in our nature, to harden ourselves within the struggle, to pick ourselves up and try again, even if ultimately we know the pursuit can never be perfected. To endure a never-ending struggle may seem exhausting, even pointless; however, there is an alternative that can also provide the humility we need, albeit in a more much dangerous fashion.

THE TRICKLE OR THE FLOOD

Is humility something you should seek out or will it eventually find you? Having made the argument humility is both direly needed and increasingly sought after in today's top leaders, this question becomes a critical one for all leaders to consider. If you decide humility is something you want to pursue, then hopefully the actions outlined in the previous chapter can be a useful guide. The choice to actively engage in a deliberate path of daily seeking is admirable. However, if this course of action appears too daunting or the price too high, understand there is also another way.

Humility is still a curious concept to most. Many leaders would readily admit they would like to be more humble but have no plan for how to move in that direction. Others may adopt a course of action but find it hard to follow. Admittedly, the path I have outlined is not an easy one to follow. It requires uncommon candor to talk openly about your mistakes and courage to intentionally insert yourself into a situation where you know you will suffer the pain and potential embarrassment of being new. However, when considering the difficulty and struggle the pursuit of humility requires, it is helpful to consider one inevitable fact. Rest assured, humility will eventually find you.

Humility is not something you want to acquire suddenly and unexpectedly after a massive failure. It is not something you want to stumble upon in the wreckage of a failed business or relationship. Humility forced upon us by stark reality is a violent act. There is a massive difference between seeking humility and being humiliated. The way we travel toward humility matters a great deal. If the persistent daily struggle to find humility is a trickle, humiliation is a dangerous, destructive flood.

Frances Perkins was the first female secretary of Labor serving in the cabinet for Franklin Delano Roosevelt throughout most of the New Deal implementation. She initially was suspicious of FDR's character but gradually came to admire the way Roosevelt gratefully and humbly accepted help. "I began to see what the great teachers of religion meant when they said that humility is the greatest of virtues," she later wrote, "and if you can't learn it, God will teach it to you by humiliation."[xxxiv]

If seeking humility can be likened to a chronic pain to endure, then humiliation is an agonizing, acute pain that cannot be contained and destroys our ability to function. To be humiliated is to be brought low by external factors, to be forcibly brought to your knees. There is often no way to soften the blow or cushion the fall. Humiliation is truly one of the cruelest forces in the universe. It robs us of joy, confidence, even hope. Mother Teresa, a model of humility and service, once said, "We learn humility through accepting humiliations cheerfully," but with great respect, this is a notion only a living saint could comprehend. While a slight faux pas may pass as a minor humiliation, true humiliation is a weight few can bear no matter how successful or strong they may seem.

Humiliation fundamentally exposes our greatest weaknesses and fears. The weakness hidden in our blind spot for years or the deep-seated fear carefully ignored. Humiliation also comes with the nasty caveat that it is very often public. To have our carefully hidden flaws laid bare can feel like drowning in shame. It is incapacitating and depressive, an overwhelmingly destructive force. If we are courageous enough to think back on a time when we felt true humiliation, the pain can still be very raw. But, despite the havoc it brings and the scars it produces, humiliation does eventually prove useful as it guides to towards humility.

When we look back on humiliations we have suffered, it is easy to be angry—to make an enemy of the person who exposed us or to second-guess the situation stacked against us. However, if we are honest, we may also admit the hard truth that we also bear a portion of responsibility. (It is worthwhile to acknowledge here that unfortunately humiliation is often brought upon innocent victims. People who suffered violence or oppression are *never* to be blamed for their terrible treatment, nor do they bear any responsibility.) As leaders, if we choose to neglect our pursuit of humility in favor of more pleasurable paths, why should be surprised when it eventually comes to visit?

We now know the power of humility. It is the antidote to arrogance; it dissipates destructive pride, and negates the self-absorption of narcissism. We now understand its power to both elevate and restore us. Humility consistently pursued and carefully cultivated over time is powerful force for good. It not only helps us sustain success but also naturally draws good people to us. It provides healthy perspective and makes us more resilient when we do face inevitable mistakes. The positive advantages of humility make a compelling case for leaders to engage in a purposeful pursuit. However, the stark reality for those still unconvinced is that humility will only be ignored for so long. And the longer we put it off, the higher the price can be.

Success in one area of life is just that—one area. Human beings are physical, mental, and spiritual beings, and health must be cultivated at each level to be truly healthy and happy. Massive success in one discipline does not mean you can ignore the others. Being a famous professional athlete cannot insulate you from the need for humility when you enter the business world. Money and wealth can build you a kingdom and buy you almost anything your heart desires. But they can't make you a good parent, a strong spouse, or even a decent human being. Even spiritual leaders must guard against a particularly insidious type of spiritual arrogance that can make them self-righteous, legalistic, and cold. Too often tremendous success in one area tricks us into thinking the same success will follow into another. Quite simply, success makes the need for humility more urgent, not less.

Blogger and spiritual advisor Vraja Bihari states the fundamental choice very eloquently: "be humble or get humbled"; the choice is yours.[xxxv] Get down on your knees voluntarily or be brought to them forcefully. David Brooks contends, "There is something morally impressive about humility." But he says the idea of engaging in a moral struggle is something we have mostly written off today. Perhaps it seems melodramatic or old-fashioned, but seeking humility requires just this type of moral struggle. We must combat our inherent selfishness and be mindful of the damaging effects success and praise can render. This struggle is not to be taken lightly, and we ignore it at our own risk.

In the end, it comes down to this: pursue humility intentionally or it will come to you eventually. Being passive and hoping humility isn't forced upon you is a highly risky strategy. Yet so many leaders unwittingly walk this path, hoping for the best as they wander toward the abyss. As a leader, there is too much at stake to take this approach. You owe it to yourself and those whom you lead to be better—to actively, intentionally engage in the struggle. As Brooks puts it, "The most important thing is whether you are willing to engage this struggle well—joyfully and compassionately." As a leader, ask yourself, "Are you willing to struggle?" To actively, even joyfully, engage in the daily struggle to become the best leader you can be?

AMPUTATING THE EGO

For the past five years, I have been honored to serve on the board of a non-profit organization called the Amputee Blade Runners (ABR). ABR was co-founded by a close friend of mine, Aaron Fitzsimmons, who worked as a prosthetist at a large surgical clinic in Nashville. Aaron is extremely talented in his expertise as a clinician and caregiver, and he is also extremely driven. Although very successful in business affairs, a few years ago he felt a strong desire to give back and serve in a more meaningful way.

There are about 200,000 amputations performed in the United States annually, and of those, nearly 80 percent are due to complications from diabetes or other chronic conditions. Seeing patients every day that have suffered the traumatic effects of an amputation, Aaron knows well the combined physical and mental struggles amputees face. Because many are older (above fifty-five) or have other complicating health factors, the rehabilitation process can be extremely difficult. Although standard health insurance provides all amputees a basic walking leg, many patients never regain the ability to walk and spend the rest of their lives in a wheelchair. Even if they happen to fall into the minority of amputees who are relatively healthy, most new amputees also struggle with depression. Having suffered a traumatic accident or life-threatening illness, most amputees find it challenging to come to terms with their new disability and worry seriously about what quality of life they will have with their new limitations. In some of the most difficult circumstances possible, amputees are literally brought to their knees. Often without warning, they are forced to engage a very real struggle to perform the basics of everyday life.

Aaron always understood the restorative power of athletics to heal both the body and mind, but the idea for ABR didn't take shape until Aaron was introduced to Ryan Fann in the spring of 2007. Ryan was finishing his degree on a track scholarship at Tennessee State University and was a testament to the impact the right equipment could have on an amputee athlete willing to put in the work. Even with a rudimentary artificial leg, Ryan was a natural athlete who started at linebacker for his high school football team. At the time he finished high school blade running legs were relatively new technology, but Ryan was lucky enough to find a sponsor to provide him with this life changing equipment for free. With his new blade leg, Ryan was soon setting new personal records on a regular basis. His hard work and improved times earned him a scholarship to run track at Tennessee State University in Nashville. Ryan eventually improved his times so dramatically that he qualified for the US Paralympic team for the 2004 games held in Athens, Greece. He won a bronze medal in the individual 400-meter race and won a gold medal as a part of the 4x400 meter relay.

After his experience in the Paralympics, Ryan became passionate about the field of prosthetics and began learning the craft working at Aaron's clinic based in Nashville. The two became training partners for an upcoming marathon and discovered they had a common passion in wanting to help other motivated amputees who had the desire to be active but couldn't afford the expensive blade running technology.

As I began working with ABR in 2011, I scaled a steep learning curve as I sought to understand the extensive medical terminology and new technology available to our amputee athletes. As I got to know them during the initial screening process, I was surprised to learn many of our amputees had actually elected to undergo voluntary amputations. To an outsider, the idea of voluntarily deciding to have a leg or foot removed seemed unfathomable. However, I soon learned that many of our ABR members struggled for years with complex birth defects that required surgery every few years as they grew. Others suffered a traumatic accident, perhaps a motorcycle wreck, and were left with mangled limbs and constant, chronic pain. The decision to amputate was especially difficult on the parents, as they often feared they would severely limit their child's lifestyle and opportunities for the future.

However, as I got to know their stories and understand their challenges better, the idea of voluntary amputation began to make sense. Most struggled mightily with the decision initially. After suffering a life-altering accident, the last thought they wanted to entertain was a permanent disability. Their initial instinct was to fight it, to think they would recover fully and the pain would eventually go away. No one wants to see their physical abilities permanently diminished, their very appearance altered forever. But over time, the pain eventually won out. Pain is persistent, pounding like the ocean. For some it would never cease, no matter what they took to numb the effects. When they finally reached the point where the physical pain was more powerful than their perceived fears for the future, most came to a place of peace with the decision to amputate.

Through their struggles to regain mobility and restore their lives, the amputee athletes of ABR certainly provide vivid examples of inspiration, determination, and pure tenacity. I have also come to marvel at their remarkable humility. The people I have met through ABR are among the most genuine and humble people you will ever come across. Despite their struggles, they are not bitter or self-pitying but rather gracious, thankful, and always looking to pay it forward to the next person. As I consider their example in the context of humility, I began to wonder if perhaps we could all benefit from a voluntary amputation of our own.

We have seen that an inflated ego brings real pain, both to others and ourselves. Dr. Silverman's work has demonstrated the damaging effects arrogance can wreak within the workplace. Deep down, we know serving our own selfish desires leads to heartache, yet we still cling to our precious egos. Like a mangled limb that only causes pain, we somehow find it hard to imagine our lives without ourselves at the center.

Imagine what it would feel like to let go of that constant striving, to forgo your ceaseless, self-serving desires? Perhaps a voluntary amputation of the ego is something we need to consider so life can take on a new, wider dimension. One that is different but inevitably improved. Lives where we can genuinely put others first, serve our organizations fully, and learn openly from our own mistakes. Brooks described egotism as "a ravenous hunger in small space—self-concerned, competitive, and distinction-hungry."[xxxvi] Ask yourself, what could I do as a leader if I were rid of this destructive hunger?

ABR was officially founded in 2011, with a mission to provide free blade running legs to active amputees across the United States. A high-performance blade can cost between $10,000 and $30,000, but because insurance companies do not consider blades to be "medically necessary", this expensive equipment is simply out of reach for many amputees. Since its inception, ABR has helped over one hundred athletes by raising funds to purchase this equipment. Aaron and Ryan meanwhile donate their time and expertise to individually fit every amputee athlete to make sure their blades fit right and enable whatever athletic dreams they may have. To learn more about their story and assist in their mission, go to www.amputeebladerunners.com.

STAYING HUMBLE

If you ever happen to hear about humility today in the popular press, is it normally mentioned when someone who has experienced success talks about the need to stay humble or perhaps to stay grounded. Tim McGraw recently had a hit on the country charts reminding us to always stay humble and kind. There is arguably no bigger entertainment star on the planet than Taylor Swift. A major reason she continues to appeal to audiences is because of her authenticity and ability to stay grounded amidst the wildly ego-swelling trappings of an A-list celebrity. Many celebrities become warped by fame. They become addicted to the roar of the crowd, the adulation from the press, and the constant deferential treatment they receive from their staff and handlers. They begin to truly think of themselves as special, unique, set apart. Honestly, who can blame them? When you are in fact a star, doesn't that entitle you to preferential treatment? Don't you get to play by a different set of rules? What is the harm in embracing it?

All you need to do is watch a single episode of *Biography* to find the answer to these questions. The celebrity fall-from-grace narrative is almost as predictable as the doomed celebrity marriage. But what is interesting about Taylor Swift is she appears to have a deliberate strategy designed to keep her ego in check. In a 2015 interview with *Extra*, Swift was asked about how she manages to stay grounded and said she studies the problems success brings and actively works to counter its destructive effects. "I would watch things like *Behind the Music* when I was growing up, and I noticed the first thing, the first step of someone's decline, in their life and in their career came when they lost perspective. When they started seeing themselves as smarter than everyone else or cooler than everyone else—or bigger, or better ... I always saw that as the biggest misstep." Others who have similarly reached the pinnacle of their profession credit their faith, family, or other trusted advisors for helping to keep their feet on the ground. Consider just these few:

- Beyoncé credits her husband, rapper Jay-Z, and her mother, Tina, for keeping her grounded when she's away from the spotlight. "Being around my family grounds me. My husband and mom are both very honest."[xxxvii]
- Apple CEO Tim Cook has an estimated net worth of over $400 million but believes living modestly keeps his ego in check. Cook resides in Palo Alto, California, in a 2,400 square foot condo that he bought for $1.9 million in 2010. In the book, *Inside Apple*, he was quoted as saying, "I like to be reminded of where I came from, and putting myself in modest surroundings helps me do that."
- Best-selling author Michael Lewis (author of *Moneyball*, *The Big Short*, and *The Blind Side*) was asked to speak to the NBA's

Golden State Warriors about how a book becomes a movie and how those at the top of their profession can strive to stay there. Lewis cited his longtime editor as a positive force. "He still looks at me [Lewis] like a twenty-six-year-old kid who sucked and is willing to tell me when me when I'm not good." This lesson caught the attention of Warriors team leader and league MVP, Steph Curry. When asked by reporters about Lewis's message, Curry replied, "He said the more he became successful, the less people wanted to tell him that, so he really cherished the couple voices around him that would keep it straight with him, no matter how big his name got, no matter how many awards he won, no matter how many best sellers he had."[xxxviii]

It takes consistent effort, awareness, and yes even some strategic focus to maintain humility. Humility is not simply a box that you can check and move on. It is not a destination at which to arrive. There is no certificate for passing the class. Just as successful individuals display a constant drive to improve their skills and push themselves toward greater levels of achievement, their needs to be a counterbalancing drive to stay hungry and stay humble.

If you are a leader, you cannot afford to be passive in cultivating humility. It needs to be a critical part of your playbook with a disciplined plan for how to periodically renew it. Taylor Swift makes it a regular practice to drop in on unsuspecting fans and deliver them birthday presents or surprise them for a special occasion. Many celebrity athletes make periodic visits to their local children's hospital to sign autographs. While these gestures are not entirely selfless (most of Taylor Swift's are accompanied by a camera crew and posted on *YouTube*), they do allow the celebrities to briefly cast themselves in the role of a servant and provide an incredible experience for the person they are meeting. Most importantly, they provide perspective, a vivid contrast showing the celebrity just how good they have it. For the celebrity, it is really a small act of kindness, but the humility it produces can be priceless.

Chapter 8

STRIKING THE BALANCE

Humility enforces where neither virtue nor
strength can prevail nor reason.
—Francis Quarles

SERVING WELL

No matter the industry, no matter the complexity or sophistication, the one chronic problem that continues to plague businesses large and small is a lack of customer service. Today most businesses within a given industry have access to the same talent, the same equipment, and similar access to technology. In such situations, the single greatest factor that can differentiate a company is their customer service (or lack thereof). From the lost bags and delayed flights of our airports, to the six-hour window for your cable company, from the cold soup, to the unintelligible operator after you have been on hold for an hour. In the twenty-first century, customer service has become the make-or-break factor for most businesses. Perhaps the most frustrating aspect is the primacy of customer service has been well established for quite some time. We already know study after study confirms the positive impact of high customer service ratings on a company's bottom line. All of which begs the question, why do so many organizations still provide such poor customer service?

Many companies have put renewed focus on driving to customer delight and are serious about tracking their Net Promoter Score (NPS), which strives to turn customers into raving fans who will actively promote their products via word of mouth and on social media. Southwest Airlines has long been the standard bearer in the airline industry because they built service into everything they do, declaring, "We like to think of ourselves as a Customer Service company that happens to fly airplanes." Others like Ritz Carlton and Disney have built their brands around providing exceptional service and see it as core to their long-term success. These companies have embedded this customer-first attitude into their cultural DNA so they select, retain, and promote people based on this strict focus. However, these companies remain the exception, not the rule. Despite others trying to duplicate their success, few have been able to follow.

At the individual level, it is also interesting to consider what factors make a person more apt to be able to delight customers versus others who may simply go through the motions. Is it temperament, talent, or skills? If we were to pick up two people off the street and take them through the Ritz Carlton's famous customer service academy, why would one thrive and the other flounder? At the individual level, are we forced to look into the mirror and ask the question, "Why is it so hard to serve well?"

It is also worth noting that all of the positive examples I have cited thus far all come from service industries where an employee typically is asked to spend a large majority of time in direct interaction with consumers. These industries typically employ large amounts of unskilled labor and seek to differentiate themselves through top-quality service. The argument could be made that they focus on customer service because their industry demands it.

But what about more technical industries like information technology, engineering, or medicine? Is there less of an expectation for highly trained individuals or technical experts when it comes to customer service? Why is that? Does technical prowess somehow trump positive customer interactions? One of the unfortunate stereotypes of surgeons is they lack the bedside manner to address patients so they prefer to deal with them once they are knocked out. Software developers suffer from a similar reputation as recalcitrant wizards best left alone to the happy clicking of their keyboards. Is there a possible correlation between highly trained professionals and an accompanying lack of customer service orientation? Is it asking too much for a highly trained expert to also engage in a positive, professional manner with customers?

I would contend that it is impossible to serve others without an intact foundation of personal humility. Acting in a professional role requiring outstanding service does not mean being submissive, passive, or even simply following orders. In fact, outstanding service is just the opposite. It is active and engaged, seeking to anticipate a customer's need and resolve it before they even inquire. It also means going beyond the stated expectation, providing the type of follow-through that is so rare it never fails to amaze and delight. It requires humility to serve well, but it also requires great confidence and the ability to step forward and accept a challenge.

The companies who continue to thrive in customer-focused service industries have realized there is great dignity and honor in serving others well. Ritz Carlton has an explicit motto that illustrates the type of anticipatory service they seek to provide. It states simply, "We are Ladies and Gentlemen serving Ladies and Gentlemen." This is brilliant because it recognizes and affirms the worth and equality of the staff is fundamental to the ability to serve well. If individuals see themselves as better, smarter, or somehow more elevated than those they serve, there is an imbalance that distorts the ability to serve. Thus the problem with highly trained individuals who feel their unique skill set puts them above those who consume their products or services. Even a tiny whiff of arrogance spoils a customer interaction every time.

Many highly trained individuals simply do not see themselves as being a part of a service industry. However, the reality is nearly everyone is afforded the opportunity to serve others. Even if you don't have direct customer interaction, you will be more successful if you have the ability to serve your boss, your colleagues, or even your children well. Great service really requires only one thing, a humble perspective recognizing that every customer has worth and dignity by virtue of their humanity. Everyone you encounter is either a lady or gentleman of value who deserves your respect and engagement. No matter your profession or discipline, the ability to serve others well is the great differentiator in business today. Ask yourself, is there anything holding you back from serving well today?

CODING FOR HUMILITY

In 1997, IBM's supercomputer Deep Blue beat legendary chess grandmaster Garry Kasparov in a head-to-head match. The victory was widely hailed as milestone breakthrough for artificial intelligence (AI) researchers but unnerved much of the general public who were distrustful of so-called, "thinking computers". Since that victory, executives at IBM continued to try to push the boundaries of AI and were looking for a new grand challenge when manager Charles Lickel proposed in 2005 that IBM begin a project to build a computer that could play the popular quiz show *Jeopardy!* Lickel had become fascinated by the record setting seventy-four-game win streak of current champion Ken Jennings and figured this type of challenge would push their research department and also potentially popularize their work. After five years of disciplined advancement and trial-and-error learning, the team felt the newly christened "Watson" was ready for prime time. The match against former champions Ken Jennings and Brad Rutter was recorded on January 14, 2011 and aired a month later. Although it failed to answer the Final Jeopardy question correctly, Watson handily won the game with $35,734 to Jennings's $4,800 and Brad Rutter's $10,400.

Watson's victory heralded significant advancements in areas like natural language processing, and this time many openly wondered if there might be more useful applications for Watson's ability to process raw data. The idea of pairing Watson with doctors to more accurately diagnose patients and keep up with the latest medical research quickly emerged. Watson's abilities were remarkable. It could consume millions of pages of medical journals and actual patient records to produce recommended treatment options ranked by order of confidence in seconds. In February 2013, IBM announced that Watson's first commercial application would be for utilization management decisions in lung cancer treatment in partnership with Memorial Sloan Kettering Cancer Center.

However, despite early positive results, there was a problem. It seemed the physicians designated to work with Watson in treating patients where not particularly fond of the know-it-all thinking computer. In his award-winning book, *The Innovators*, Walter Isaacson indicated physicians particularly disliked the way it presented diagnosis recommendations with virtual certainty. While IBM programmers felt strongly their information was accurate, they struggled with how to gain the physicians' trust to ensure the proposed collaboration would actually benefit patients.

Their solution was to try to program humility into Watson so the recommendations to physicians would come across more as suggestions than commands. David McQueeney, vice president of software at IBM, reported, "We reprogrammed our system to come across as humble and say, 'Here's the percentage likelihood that this is useful to you, and here's where you can look for yourself.'" Today, IBM continues to spawn multiple programs seeking to combine the judgment and clinical expertise of physicians with the computational, data-crunching power of Watson. Despite the technically wizardry of Watson, the computer was not able to serve patients well until the programmers introduced synthetic humility into the solution to enable better collaboration.

The simple lesson is one you probably learned in kindergarten—nobody likes a know-it-all. But it is a powerful one for any advanced professional to consider. Rarely is being the best doctor or computer programmer simply a matter of technical skill or knowledge. Almost all great accomplishments are done in collaboration. What if your superior talent or knowledge is actually a hindrance to effective collaboration and may be holding you back? This means you may never truly maximize your talents and accomplish your best work. Watson has already bested humans at *Jeopardy!* Surely if a supercomputer can utilize the power of humility to become more effective, then we as humans can rediscover its transformational power as well.

HUMILITY PLUS ...

In my obsessive, ongoing quest to unlock the power of humility for leaders, I have also come to realize one fundamental truth. Humility alone is not enough. Although I am fully convinced of its power and significance, I also have come to understand it does not stand alone. Humility alone is not always the answer, but humility does have the power to help us find the answer. Let's review for a minute what we have learned in the previous chapters:

- In *Good to Great*, Jim Collins and his team opened our eyes to the power of humility. They recognized it as the capstone of a leader's journey and explained it was the particular pairing of humility with intense professional will that made the difference for their Level 5 leaders who grossly outperformed their more egocentric competitors.
- During his fascinating study of survival specialists in high-risk professions, Laurence Gonzales demonstrated it was an exceptional balance of boldness and humility that allowed naval aviators and astronauts to remain sharp and perceive situations clearly even under the stress of life-and-death decisions.
- Pope Francis through his personal style and professed leadership philosophy has provided a contemporary example of how to balance sincere service with any ability to assertively challenge the status quo in one of the world's most insular organizations.

In exploring this wide diversity of styles and circumstances, we have seen the broad power of humility to transform, protect, and enhance.

It is interesting to consider that despite the wide variety of personalities and situations, the common theme has been to pair humility with its seemingly opposite trait to produce the most effective results. Need to land a jet fighter on an aircraft carrier in the dark of night? Pair a strong dose of *Top Gun* moxie with just the right amount of humility. Want to shake up an arrogant, bloated bureaucracy? Combine equal parts of creativity and courage with a healthy dose of humility. Need to take the next step in your career and earn that big promotion? Move forward aggressively with an equal mixture of confidence and humility to produce results and make allies along the way. In the end, these recipe-like metaphors seem to strike the right balance and produce results, but is it really that simple?

F. Scott Fitzgerald once declared, "The sign of a first-rate intelligence is the ability to hold two opposing ideas in the mind at the same time and still retain the ability to function." This sentiment rings true as we struggle to understand how a well-trained Navy Seal can be equal parts bold warrior and humble servant. Navy Seals are displaying this first-rate intelligence and have seemingly mastered this difficult blend. Harvard Professor Gautam Mukunda underscores Fitzgerald's idea in his excellent leadership study, *Indispensable,* by suggesting great leaders are those who are able to "reject a false choice and create a new option."[xxxix] In seeking to define what separates a truly great leader, Mukunda states explicitly they "are able to mix the two seemingly opposite character traits—extreme humility and extreme self-confidence." He says it is the unique ability to be "resolute enough to reject advice and uncertain enough to take it," but most importantly, "somehow they know when they should be each."

His line of thought parallels our previous supposition regarding the balance of opposites but highlights the important power of choice in knowing which to apply and when. We can even hear echoes of this thinking in the famous Serenity Prayer that has helped generations of those struggling with addiction to find the humility to accept the things they cannot change, the courage the change the things they can, and the crucial wisdom to know the difference. Noted Jewish author and spiritual advisor Nilton Bonder sums it up saying, "Many people believe that humility is the opposite of pride, when, in fact, it is a point of equilibrium."

However, I would contend that even this simple metaphor of balance is incomplete. The idea of balance is an incomplete because it incorrectly pits humility in opposition to some other equally desirable quality or virtue. Humility versus confidence or humility as opposed to boldness. It implies humility and ambition cannot coexist—as if humility sits on one side of the scale competing for supremacy against another necessary good. There is a very natural human tendency to simplify, to see things in binary options (i.e., on or off, black or white), or to simply pit good against evil. Although understandable, none of these metaphors are appropriate when it comes to humility. Humility is not the opposite of confidence. It doesn't somehow diminish the need for confidence in leadership.

If we go back to the opening question I asked in chapter 1 about which executive (A or B) you would prefer to have running your company, we can now recognize the question was rigged. Many of you may have thought, *why can't I choose a leader that is both dynamic and aggressive but also gracious and humble?* By setting up humility in opposition to these other desirable qualities of leadership, we have made it too easy for humility to be neglected, ignored, and devalued. We have turned it into a binary choice between one or the other. Without intention, we have unfortunately created the type of false choice Mukunda warned against. By doing so, we relegate this complicated balancing act to something only elite leaders or those who possess truly first-rate intelligence can hope to achieve. A small minority of CEOs, Navy Seals, or a once-in-a-lifetime pontiff. By making humility a mystical quality only a few can achieve, we have done all leaders a disservice. Unwittingly, we have also made it much more likely leaders will choose to pursue the other side of the scale, as surely confidence and assertiveness may be grasped more easily than the hard-to-hold nature of humility.

At the end, I would hope you can see past this false choice and realize humility is something very much within your grasp. While it may not come easily to many, it *can* be sought after, cultivated, and improved with the same diligence and effort we would apply to other important endeavors worth pursuing. It will not damage your confidence, take away your drive, or cause you to lose to more ambitious competitors. In fact, it makes you stronger, more resilient, and sets you up better for long-term, balanced success in multiple areas of your life and work.

THE RESOLUTION OF LINCOLN

If you've ever had the chance to visit Washington, DC, and walk the National Mall, you have very likely climbed the majestic steps of the Lincoln Memorial. Inscribed on the wall to President Lincoln's left are the words of his second inaugural address. The speech was given on March 4, 1865 when the bloody struggle of civil war was within days of ending, and yet in a moment when Lincoln could have rightly boasted, he instead struck a somber, pragmatic tone.

> Neither party expected for the war the magnitude or the duration which it has already attained. Neither anticipated that the cause of the conflict might cease with, or even before, the conflict itself should cease. Each looked for an easier triumph, and a result less fundamental and astounding. Both read the same Bible, and pray to the same God; and each invokes his aid against the other. It may seem strange that any men should dare to ask a just God's assistance in wringing their bread from the sweat of other men's faces; but let us judge not, that we be not judged.

Lincoln then really hits his stride when he eloquently discussed the moral struggle of the nation to end slavery and how the lives lost in the horrible conflict might perhaps have been the sacrifice that could ultimately redeem the nation.

> Fondly do we hope—fervently do we pray—that this mighty scourge of war may speedily pass away. Yet, if God wills that it continue until all the wealth piled by the bondman's two hundred and fifty years of unrequited toil shall be sunk, and until every drop of blood drawn with the lash shall be paid by another drawn with the sword, as was said three thousand years ago, so still it must be said, "The judgments of the Lord are true and righteous altogether."

But it is the last few lines Mukunda says that perfectly illustrate both the resolution and humble openness the very best leaders need to possess.

> With malice toward none; with charity for all; with firmness in the right, as God gives us to see the right, let us strive on to finish the work we are in …

As leaders, we will always need the resolution to do what is right, what is hard, what is unpopular. We need the confidence to boldly proceed and execute our mission. Humility strengthens leaders, providing perspective and checking the inherent power leadership provides with the willingness to admit that one cannot see fully. Humble leaders are comfortable wielding power but are always judicious in its use. Lincoln's words ring true today just as they did then. May we also have the courage and resolution to purse what is right but be smart enough to realize our perspective is never entirely accurate. There is always more to learn, and we must be active and tenacious in our pursuit. More than ever, the world needs leadership. Not the cheap, self-serving, ego-driven leadership of the charismatic leader but the bold, confident, and humble leadership Lincoln displayed.

PERSPECTIVE AT FORTY AU

On September 5, 1977, the Voyager 1 probe was launched from Launch Complex 41 at the Cape Canaveral Air Force Station. Probe's primary mission was to explore the planets Jupiter and Saturn, and Saturn's large moon, Titan. The mission proceeded well, and Voyager 1 began photographing Jupiter in January 1979. In addition to the spectacular images Voyager captured, the most dramatic discovery was the evidence of volcanic activity on Jupiter's moon named Io. It was the first time active volcanoes had been seen on another body in the solar system and caused a great stir among the scientific community. However, Voyager 1 has become even better known for the last photograph it would take on February 14, 1990.

The idea was to capture a family portrait of our solar system by turning the Voyager 1 around and snapping a series of images from a record distance of about six billion kilometers or forty astronomical units (AU) from Earth. The picture is actually a mosaic of sixty individual frames capturing six planets, including Jupiter, Earth, Venus, Saturn, Uranus, and Neptune. The sun is also visible as a point of light in the distance. The idea for the photograph was hatched by the Voyager team and campaigned hard for by astronomer Carl Sagan, who later wrote a masterful essay based on the images entitled "The Pale Blue Dot."

> From this distant vantage point, the Earth might not seem of any particular interest. But for us, it's different. Consider again that dot. That's here. That's home. That's us. On it everyone you love, everyone you know, everyone you ever heard of, every human being who ever was, lived out their lives. The aggregate of our joy and suffering, thousands of confident religions, ideologies, and economic doctrines, every hunter and forager, every hero and coward, every creator and destroyer of civilization, every king and peasant, every young couple in love, every mother and father, hopeful child, inventor and explorer, every teacher of morals, every corrupt

politician, every "superstar," every "supreme leader," every saint and sinner in the history of our species lived there—on a mote of dust suspended in a sunbeam.

The Earth is a very small stage in a vast cosmic arena. Think of the rivers of blood spilled by all those generals and emperors so that in glory and triumph they could become the momentary masters of a fraction of a dot. Think of the endless cruelties visited by the inhabitants of one corner of this pixel on the scarcely distinguishable inhabitants of some other corner. How frequent their misunderstandings, how eager they are to kill one another, how fervent their hatreds. Our posturings, our imagined self-importance, the delusion that we have some privileged position in the universe, are challenged by this point of pale light. Our planet is a lonely speck in the great enveloping cosmic dark. In our obscurity— in all this vastness—there is no hint that help will come from elsewhere to save us from ourselves.

Shortly after snapping the family portrait of our universe, Voyager 1's cameras were deactivated to conserve power. Now, having operated for more than thirty-eight years, the probe is still able to communicate with the Deep Space Network, and as of spring 2017, it is the farthest spacecraft from Earth and the only one in interstellar space.

More than anything else, the essence of humility can be summed up in one word: perspective. The ability to accurately see ourselves from a distance without the haze and distortion ego inevitably causes. Just imagine what we could do—do differently, do better, if we were able to continually hone this perspective. To occasionally turn around and get a snapshot of how far we have come and how much we still have left to do. In the end, humility may not be a perfect tool, it may not be able to provide the scientific precision of a spacecraft, but it is readily available for those who have the courage and persistence to seek it.

ACKNOWLEDGMENTS

For many, the genesis of humility is found in gratitude. Understanding that we have been blessed and that our meager efforts are only a small part of the equation leads us down the path to humility. I agree, and I am profoundly grateful to many people for their support, encouragement, and faith as I took on this adventure.

First and foremost is my high school sweetheart, my prom date, my forever one-and-only, Ashlie. You have always been my cheerleader and have grown to be my most trusted partner. Thank you for building me up and for encouraging me when I needed it. You are my heart. I also need to thank Wallace, Emory, and Anderson for keeping the house quiet on Saturday mornings as I tried to find time to write. You all bring me so much joy and gratitude. Thank you for listening to my first version of the Humility Advantage and for giving me hope that our next generation may also know and value humility.

I was exceedingly fortunate to grow up with exceptional, hardworking parents who always supported me and continue to do so today. Their unwavering support and selfless love molded my character. As a child, my single greatest motivation was really just to make my parents proud. Things are not so different today, so I hope you all enjoy this book and know that I am who I am today because of you all. Thanks to my brother, Addison, and my sisters, Anna, Amanda, and April, for their lifetime of support and enthusiasm.

Next I want to thank all my friends and colleagues that provided feedback and encouraged me to make this book a reality. The list is long but probably starts with my mentors and supporters at HCA.

Thank you for allowing me to teach leadership classes for so many years, even while I was learning lessons on the job. It starts with Becky and Marty Paslick who brought me into the company and continues down to great friends like Debye Leahy, Sheila Stern, Chris Pair, Donita Brown, Andre Ballew, Kenny Hilpp, Laura Kinnard, Leah Miller, and Chris Mott. Special thanks goes to Sheila Gibson who gave me my first-ever opportunity to teach the Humility Advantage at the annual EEOG leadership conference. Sarah Richardson is also due special thanks for being an advanced reader of my manuscript and providing great tips for edits and revisions. Your support has always given me great confidence, and I have always learned by watching you lead. Another special note of thanks to Alisha Klapheke for her candid advice and review of my manuscript. You are a much better writer than I will ever be, so thanks for willingly sharing your professional expertise with this rookie!

My late grandfather, Ed Lord, literally taught me what the word "modest" meant one day as we drove through Atlanta and for some reason, I have always remembered it. I want to thank all the leaders that I have had the privilege to study up close. This list starts with my father and extends out to Ed McGuire, former Vanderbilt head coach Bobby Johnson, my friend John McConnell, Noel Williams, Marty Paslick, and Tim Unger. Thanks for sharing your wisdom and your struggles.

Lastly, good friends are hard to find. Good friends keep you humble and also are always there to help you celebrate! Thanks to Dean, Nathan, Wally, John, Brandt, Logan, Duane, and Aaron.

NOTES

Chapter 1

[i]   Ronald Shelp, *Fallen Giant: The Amazing Story of Hank Greenberg and the History of AIG,* (Wiley: 2009), 248.

[ii]   Jim Collins, *Good To Great,* (2001), 20.

[iii]   "Sir Galahad," *Complete Poetical Works of Tennyson,* 101.

[iv]   Friedrich Nietzsche, *Twilight of the Idols* (1889).

[v]   David Brooks, *The Road to Character* (2015), 6.

[vi]   P.J. Kesebir, "A quiet ego quiets death anxiety: humility as an existential anxiety buffer," *Pers Soc Psychol* 106, no. 4 (April 2014): 610–23, doi: 10.1037/a0035814.

[vii]   Ronald Shelp, *Fallen Giant: The Amazing Story of Hank Greenberg and the History of AIG* (Wiley: 2009).

[viii]   James Stewart, "Hank Greenberg still in the Ring at 90, Battling AIG Charges," *New York Times* (April 30, 2016).

Chapter 2

[ix]   Rich Exner, "Success for quarterbacks picked in NFL Draft first round? Less than 50-50, even for highest picks," Cleveland.com (April 28, 2015).

[x]   Thomas Friedman, "How to Get a Job at Google," *New York Times* (2/22/14).

[xi]   Michael Johnson, University of Washington Foster School of Business.

[xii]   Bradley P Owens, David R Hekman, "Modeling how to grow: An inductive examination of humble leader behaviors, contingencies, and outcomes," *Academy of Management Journal* 55, no. 48 (December 2012): 787–818.

[xiii]   Daryl R. Van Tongerena*, Don E. Davisb & Joshua N. Hook, "Social benefits of humility: Initiating and maintaining romantic relationships," *Journal of Positive Psychology* 9, no. 4 (2014): 313–321.

Chapter 3

[xiv] Mark Binelli, "Pope Francis: The Times They Are A-Changin'", *Rolling Stone Magazine* (1/28/14).

[xv] Jim Harter, Amy Adkins, "State of the American Manager: Analytics and Advice for Leaders," *Gallup.com* (4/8/15).

[xvi] Patrick Lencioni, *The Advantage* (2012), 26-27.

[xvii] Adam Bryant, *The Corner Office: Indispensable and Unexpected Lessons from CEOs on How to Lead and Succeed* (2012).

[xviii] Carol Dweck, *Mindset: The New Psychology of Success* (2007).

Chapter 4

[xix] Laurence Gonzales, *Deep Survival: Who Lives, Who Dies, and Why* (2004).

[xx] Eric Johnson, "Why Narcissistic CEOs Kill Their Companies," *Forbes* (January 11, 2012).

[xxi] Marshall Goldsmith, *What Got You Here Won't Get You There: How Successful People Become Even More Successful* (2007).

Chapter 5

[xxii] Anne Casselman, "10 Biggest Oil Spills in History," *Popular Mechanics*, (May 7, 2010).

[xxiii] Peter Firestein, *Crisis of Character—Building Corporate Reputation in the Age of Skeptics* (2009).

[xxiv] Gus Chazan, "Tony Hayward, Genel Energy CEO: now he has his life back," *The Financial Times* (September 14, 2014).

[xxv] Stanley Reed, "Tony Hayward Gets His Life Back," *The New York Times* (9/1/12).

[xxvi] Steve Coll, "Barrage of Bullets Drowned Out Cries of Comrades," *The Washington Post* (12/5/04).

Chapter 6

[xxvii] John Krakauer, *Where Men Win Glory: The Odyssey of Pat Tillman* (2010).

[xxviii] Richard Lacayo, "The Death of a Volunteer - One For the Team," *Time Magazine* (5/3/04).

[xxix] Matthew Hutson, "Why Oscar Winners Say They're 'Humbled'". *The Atlantic* (3/2/14).

[xxx] Matthew Syed, *Black Box Thinking: Why Most People Never Learn from Their Mistakes--But Some Do* (2015).

[xxxi] Amy Cuddy, "Your body language shapes who you are" *Ted.com*, June 2012.

xxxii   Jay Van Bavel, "The Dark Side of Power Posing: Cape or Kryptonite?" *Scientific American* (11/21/13).

Chapter 7

xxxiii Bill Wilson, *The Best of Bill: Reflections on Faith, Fear, Honesty, Humility, and Love* (1990).
xxxiv   David Brooks, *The Road to Character* (2015), 40.
xxxv   Blog: Yoga for the Modern Age by Vraja Bihari Das, May 6, 2014 http://yogaformodernage.com/be-humble-or-get-humbled/
xxxvi   David Brooks, *The Road to Character* (2015), 8.
xxxvii Beyonce on 'Today': Staying grounded and 'Jersey Shore', *Examiner.com* (2/9/10).
xxxviii Chris Ballard, "Inside Warriors practices: Laughs, lessons and a little basketball," *Sports Illustrated.com* (3/23/16).

Chapter 8

xxxix   Gautam Mukunda, *Indispensable*, (2015)

ABOUT THE AUTHOR

Andrew Kerr is a technology executive with more than ten years of diverse experience leading teams, delivering solutions, and helping individuals and organizations to grow and thrive. He is the CEO FortyAU, LLC, where he leads a team of software developers that delivers custom software solutions in the health care, higher education, sports, and entertainment industries. He also teaches dozens of classes on various topics, including change management, managing up, lateral leadership, and the power of humility for leaders. He lives with his wife, Ashlie, and their three energetic children in Franklin, Tennessee.

ABOUT THE AUTHOR

Want to book Andrew to speak at your next event?

The *Humility Imperative* class is available as a 90-minute onsite training session that delivers high impact results for your team. This one-of-a-kind facilitated session will bring the power of humility to work for your team!

Please send all inquires to: HumilityImperative@gmail.com or follow Andrew on Twitter @AndrewKerr11